# On Foe'nem Grave: Book (1)

## Best Kept Secret

# On Foe'nem Grave: Book (1)
# Best Kept Secret

By Makaroni Montana

*So You Can Write Publications, LLC*
*PO Box 80736*
*Milwaukee, WI 53208*
*www.sycwp.com*

*Copyright © 2022 Makaroni Montana*
*All rights reserved*

*No part of this book may be reproduced, or stored in a retrieval system, or transmitted in any form or by any means, electronic, mechanical, photocopying, recording, or otherwise, without express written permission of the publisher.*

*Publishing date: 12/19/2022*
*ISBN-13: 978-1-7376084-8-6*

*Cover design by: www.sycwp.com*
*Printed in the United States of America*

*(Note: "The majority of quotations gathered by the author have been frequently in print and/or movie and television, as well as publicly accessible on the Internet; considered public domain. Where possible, the author and publisher have made their best efforts to credit any available sources for them. In the cases where it was uncertain where they first appeared, the information was cited as "unknown" or "anonymous." The information in this book is intended to uplift and inspire all who read it, or who have it read to them. The information quoted was kept as it was found and/or heard by the author, who makes no guarantee that the information one-hundred percent accurate, just that the author intended for it to be beneficial to all who reads it, or has it read to them."*

# Dedication

I would first like to thank God for giving me the ability to write, to have patients, and to stay focused. It has truly been a blessing. I would like to dedicate this book to my mother. You were my everything. You always taught me how not to settle, and that anything is possible. You are truly missed. I think about you every day, but I promise to be all that I could be and continue to make you proud. Everything I do I do it knowing you're looking down watching over me, my guardian angel. Love you and until we meet again you will forever be in my heart, rest up. To my best friend Stevo…. rest up lil bruh, shit will never be the same without you. Also, I want to say rest in peace to the guys: PO, AK, Calvo, Kenny, Chris, Jessica, Big Bud, Money Mel, and my nigga Bullet, rest in Paradise.

# Chapter (1)

**M**usic could be heard from distances away; the latest and hottest songs were being mixed by the DJ. Club "Secrets" was in full swing, everybody that was somebody were in attendance. A block away checking his 17-shot baby 9mm. was Valo. He made sure that it was off safety and one was in the chamber. He always felt it was better to be safe than sorry. Usually, he would take his Glock because it didn't have any safety, but in this case his twin brother Flo beat him to the punch. Flo being the oldest by two minutes was by far the most ruthless young savage in Dade county. The fear he put in most men kept them above water.

That was off his reputation alone. He literally scared the shit outta most men in his area. Rumor has it that he was responsible for more than 10 bodies this year alone and it was only August. Valo was more of a thinker, he always thought something through before he reacted. He knew something had to give, he knew he needed to become a real man, Sasha always told him a man who don't work don't eat. He was grateful that Jade stuck by him through everything, she was his heart and he promised her that one day he'll give her the world. At 20, both men were a product of the streets.

Their story is kind of shaky, but it was told to them that they mom died in the delivery room giving birth to them. They were also told that their father was against her having them, but she refused to abort her miracle babies.

"Nope, not my babies, I'd rather die before I do some shit like that." She later died on the delivery table.

Kane, their father walked away not even bothering to take a look at the boys blaming them for their mother's death.

"How can she choose some kids she never met over me?" he asked himself time after time. With no one to claim them, the twins were later adopted.

"Bruh, you sure this nigga in this muthafucka club?" Flo ask in an anxious irritated voice. Flo who was always ready to bust his gun was tired of sitting and waiting in their raggedy ass ford explorer. One of the cars that the Feds didn't take from the family when they came and apprehended Sasha. Sasha was the boys foster mother. At the age of 43 years old, 5'6, 135lbs proportion in all the right places, Columbia and black; Sasha could be any men biggest strength or biggest weakness. She was as beautiful as can be, she was very dark with Cuban hair which gave her that exotic look. She looked like she was in her late twenty's more than her early 40s. She was the only mother that the boys knew and they loved her with every fiber in their bones. She raised them since they were barley one years old. It wasn't easy and it wasn't hard, it was simply a dream come true. Shit haven't been the same for the twins since she went away.

The two boys felt lost most of the time. Sasha was sentenced to 20 years in the feds for conspiracy to distribute 10 kilos of pure Columbia Coke. The feds took everything but the Ford. To be quite frank, it wasn't worth shit anyway.

"Showtime," Valo whispered excitingly. "Dats dat fuck nigga right there with the two bitches on his arm," Valo assured.

"About to get in the Rover?" Flo asked anxiously. Turning quickly, Flo grab the inside of the car door handle ready to hop out and kidnap his ass. He stopped in his tracks once he felt Valo grab his arm.

"Fuck you doing bruh?" Valo whisper harshly.

"Fuck you think bruh? I'm about to go snatch this fuck nigga up so he can take us to the stash house." Flo countered angrily.

"Look my boy," Valo said in a calm demeanor. "We went over this shit ten times, we just gone follow the bitch nigga to his spot, that way we can get everything at once and won't be no witnesses if we have to smoke his ass."

"You mean when we smoke his ass, we not robbing no nigga and leaving him alive," Flo replied evilly. Flo who was tired of being the lil niggas on the block that the bad bitches wouldn't give no play. He was ready to eat, he was ready to prove himself, he was ready to be like his momma… 'A real muthafucken gangsta…' Most boys wanted be like their father, not Flo, he never even had one. He wanted to be like his mother, a certified Drug Lord that stood ten toes down on the streets of Miami. She ran her shit with an iron fist.

Pulling out, Valo blew out a frustrated breath.

"Yeah, bruh, when we smoke his ass," Valo agreed. Valo began to navigated the ford carefully behind the Rover keeping a safe distance away from the beautiful foreign. "This nigga must be drunk bruh because he swerving like a muthafucka," Valo complained more to himself then to his better half.

"That's good, that mean his ass gone be easy to take down," Flo replied with no remorse. "Or harder, you know how drunk muthafuckas don't be in their right state of mind," Flo reasoned. Pulling into a beautiful small section of South beach, Florida suburban area and parking down the block, Flo noticed how their raggedy ass Ford stuck out like a thick stripper bitch booty cheek. "Man, lets rob the whole fucking block!" Flo suggested in amazement. "You see all these muthafucken foreign cars on this block mane?" Flo asked seriously.

Laughing, Valo looked at his twin, "You can't be serious bruh?" The look on Flo face told it all, he was indeed serious, serious as a heart attack. Shaking his head chuckling Valo begin putting the mask over his face making sure he tucked his shoulder length dreadlocks in his shirt. He was happy he let Tiffany, his thick ass down stairs neighbor braid his shit. Standing at 6'2, about 215lbs, dark brown skin, fine was an understatement for the twins. Women loved the smooth skin and perfect teeth the twins possessed. Not to mention, they worked out at home regularly. The only problem was they were broke, but hopefully that shit was all about to change. Valo, who had been planning and lurking on this mark for a month straight finally felt that tonight was the night. He felt it was time to get his money up, that it was time to boss the fuck up. The twins were identical, the only way Sasha was able to tell them apart when they were young was one of them was left handed and the other was right handed. Taking note, Flo begin pulling his mask over his face, also tucking his dreads.

"You ready bro?"

"Yeah," Valo said heart thumbing out his chest. Easing out of the car the boys could see their mark staggering toward his house without a care in the world.

"Which one of you hoes gone suck daddy dick first?" The mark asked in a drunken slur, standing about 5'7 and 280lbs, he was definitely fat as hell.

"How about we do it at the same time?" one of the strippers cooed. Fumbling with the keys the strippers had the mark lil dick hard as a jolly rancher. When entering the home, the mark aggressively pushes the strippers into the living room.

"You bitches dance for me," the mark demanded turning on the music. Suddenly hearing the music, the strippers jumped into mode and began dancing, shaking they jiggly asses in his face. They just knew a big payday was coming because Jimbo was a well-known baller and he loved tricking off with young bitches.

"Bruh, this gone be sweeter than we thought, this dumb ass muthafucka left the door open," Flo confirmed twisting the nob.

"Yeah?" Valo asked coming behind Flo, "Let's go then bruh." Entering the home, they could hear the music and the strippers laughing. Guns leading the way as the twins followed the voices. Laying on the sofa with a bitch on his face and one riding his dick the mark was in heaven. The twins stood there undetected for a whole thirty second enjoying the show.

"Enough!" Flo barked grabbing the smaller stripper by her hair yanking and throwing her to the floor catching them completely off guard. Sobering up quickly, the mark sat up reaching for his strap instantly cursing himself for getting caught slipping and leaving his guns in the car.

'I knew I should of just went home…' the mark thought regretfully. He knew his wife was at home taking care of their new born son and here he was with two stripper bitches he barely knew trying to get his freak on. Not to mention, he was in the stash house his wife knew nothing about. He vowed that if he got out of this he was gone do right by his wife and child.

"Oh, my God don't kill me!" the taller stripper began screaming.

"Shut the fuck up bitch and lay yo ass on the floor before I push yo shit back, all you muthafuckas," Flo demanded.

"Man, the work in the deep freezer and the money is between the mattress," Jimbo confessed spilling his guts.

"If you lying you a dead man," Valo barked quickly leaving to check it out. Running to the kitchen Valo spotted the deep freezer instantly. He quickly began throwing things out until he discovers the two bricks of China White and three pounds of Jalatto kush. Quickly running to the room, he spotted the bed and flipped over the mattress discovering two AR's, a Draco, a F&N, and a gold 9mm. Valo looked at the 9mm. with admiration.

*'Prince gone love this bitch…'* he thought before tucking it in his waste, he still couldn't find the money though. Valo ran back into the front room angry. "Where the fuck the money at bitch nigga?" Valo asked.

"I swear it's in the mattress," Jimbo pleaded.

"Awe, okay you wanna lie to my brother?" Flo asked getting excited; **Boom Boom Boom!** Flo shot the taller stripper three times killing her instantly.

"Oh, my gosh my sister oh, my gosh my sister!" the shorter stripper cried. Flo aim the Glock at the shorter stripper, "Please, I'm only 17!" **Boom Boom Boom Boom**, he shot her four times silencing her forever.

"You wanna lie to my fucken brother huh B?" Flo screamed vexed. Flo spotted a hammer on the shelf then grabbed it and approach the mark; **wack wack wack**.

"Ahhhhh!" Jimbo screamed. Flo hit him repeatedly in his pelvis area.

"Shut yo bitch ass up," Flo smiled amused. "Now, where that shit at Money?" he asked again.

"I told you it was in between the mattress, I promise man, I wouldn't lie to you, that shit isn't worth my life. I got a son, I just had him please don't kill me man!" the mark pleaded holding his groin area. Valo ran back to the room and began feeling in between the mattress.

*'Jack pot…'* he thought to his self as he felt a different type of pattern in the thread of the mattress. He began throwing stack after stack of money into the duffel bag. Arriving back in the living room he spotted his twin standing over the mark repeatedly smashing the hammer into his face.

**Wack-** "You want to," **Wack-** "lie," **Wack-** "to my brother!" **Wack- Wack- Wack- Wack**.

*'What the fuck?'* Valo thought froze. "Bro let's roll!" Valo grabbed Flo's arm snapping him outta his trend. "I got the shit," Valo announced with a disgusted look on his face like he was about to throw up. Most of the mark face was caved in and all you could see was jaw bone and nose bone, even his eye balls were smashed in. Flo looked up with a crazy look on his face.

"Where you find it at?" he asked confused.

"It was where he said it was, between the mattresses. I looked under it at first and not in between them," Valo replied.

"So yo bitch ass did tell the truth huh?" Flo asked the dead man with a slight chuckle. "My bad, you should've been more specific," he told the dead man picking up the hammer with no remorse.

"Wipe down everything you touched, bro we out this bitch," Valo said in a panicked voice. Looking at the mess his brother made he began to wonder was the rumors about his brother true; were these bodies eleven, twelve, and thirteen? Did his twin kill thirteen people this year???

# Chapter (2)

The irritating sound of Flo's iPhone woke him outta his weed induced coma. He felt like he'd just dosed off, slowly opening his eyes he tried to come to his senses. His mind was still racing from the excitement of the lick from last night. It was hands down the biggest score ever for the twins and he couldn't sleep worth shit. Not to mention, that they spent half of the night cooking up the two kilos that they came up on from the move. They were anxious to put the product out in the streets, he was ready to eat. He saw his momma take over the streets and he plan on doing the same thing, no question about it. They also put pink dye in the dope so the customers could know when it's their dope to assure them that it's the same product. Sometimes they would switch colors, an old trick they learned from Sasha. Thanks to Sasha and Pops, one of the neighborhood junkies that use to cook up for Sasha, they had the best whip game all the way from Dade to Orange County. Grabbing his phone waking up groggy, Flo sleepily answered, "Hello?"

"You have a collect call from Sandy Federal Correctional institution at no expense to you from Sasha Fearis. To accept press 5." Hearing his momma on the line woke him all the way up with a smile on his face. He set up in the bed and pressed 5 quickly listening to the operator before hearing his Mother soft sweet voice.

"Hello? Hey ma, how you holding up?" Flo asked with concern evident in his tone.

"Hey Flo baby, mama doing good, as best as I can be under these circumstances. This fucking Covid shutting every fucking thing down, plus they keep coming out with new strains of Covid, I feel like the fucking world is about to end. But trust me, these assholes know not to fuck with me here, they can have my body but they can never have my mind." Sasha replied in a gangsta way. "What have you guys been up to? I haven't been able to reach you guys in a few days." Sasha asked in a curious tone.

"Yeah, I know ma," Flo paused, "me and Valo have been kinda busy with a lot of things, shit been rough but now it's getting better."

"Did y'all make that move?"

"Yeah, ma, I took care of it personally."

"Okay, sounds good."

"How are your books looking?" Flo asked.

"Am I missing something?" Sasha replied making a face.

"No," Flo replied to quickly for Sasha's taste, but she just left it alone for now. "Well, I guess it's gone get better, today me and Valo got sum for you," Flo stated excitedly.

"Oh, really?" Sasha replied in a surprise voice.

"Yeah, ma, we been making big moves," he bragged. "So, hopefully we can get that lawyer to try and get your conviction overturned," he continued.

"Sounds good to me," Sasha replied all smiles. She was used to hearing her boys dream about how they were going to get her lawyer to get her sentence over turned. Lord knows the Feds did her dirty, she wasn't even caught with anything and they never revealed the confidential informant. "Speaking of Valo, where is your brother?" she asked.

"Hold on ma, let me wake him up," Flo stated jumping up.

"No, don't bother. I'll call y'all back later just be on point."

*"All calls other than properly place attorney calls may be monitor and recorded,"* the operator interrupted.

"I have to go son, I love you; tell Valo I love him and I'll call again soon."

"Okay ma, we gone have some money on your books today okay?" Flo promised.

"Okay baby, I'll talk to you later," Sasha replied before hanging up the phone.

Sitting up Flo looked around his small room in his rundown apartment he shared with his brother, it wasn't in either of the boys' names. The landlord was a pure crack head, he was even rumored to sometimes accept Food Stamps for payment. Flo smiled once he noticed the stack of money sitting on the dresser. Sixty-thousand-dollars split in two way was by far the most money the twins have ever had in their entire life, on their own. Thinking about the events that took place he smiled even harder.

"Lil bruh came through with this lick," he whispers to himself. *'I can't wait to buy Jade something nice...'* he thought. Feeling the need to smoke some of the fire Jalatto kush they came up on,

Flo got out the bed and headed to the living room. Not finding any back woods to smoke out of, Flo walked to Valo's room and eased his door open. "Yo bruh, you got some back woods in this bitch?" Flo yelled loud enough to stir Valo outta his sleep.

"Nawl bruh," Valo replied irritated. He too, felt like he just went to sleep.

"Okay, imma run to the corner store, you want anything," Flo asked?

"Yeah, bruh, grab me an orange juice or sum," Valo yond.

"Mom called too," Flo said cutting him off.

"What?" Valo sat up quickly, "what she say?" he questioned surprised that his twin didn't wake him up.

"Shit, just that she'll call back later and she loves you."

"You tell her we gone send her some bread and shit?"

"Yeah," Flo replied. "She sounded good, a lil skeptical though.

"Well, shit I can't blame her, how many times we told her we going to do sum knowing damn well we didn't have a penny to our names," Valo reasoned.

"Yeah, well, shit about to change now though with the way we got this work and shit whipped, we gone be fucking Kings of Miami bruh."

"I sure hope so," Valo replied hopeful.

"Trust me bruh, today is the first day of the rest of our lives," Flo stated with passion. "Your phone been blowing up bruh all fucking night, how you sleep through that shit, isn't that shit annoying?" Flo asked.

"Man, that shit isn't easy but you know if I turn my phone off Jade gone lose her fucking mind," Valo stated.

"Yeah, I know, she is a wild one. I'll be back though, I'm out." Grabbing some money and the bag of thirty-ten-dollar testers that he plans on passing out, Flo left and headed out the door.

The sun was shining, it felt like at least 95' degrees out. The block was already in full swing at 11am. Walking down the block crossing the alley Flo spotted Lea, one of Sasha old friends. "Lea!" Flo yell gaining her attention. Recognizing him instantly Lea began walking toward him seductively.

"What's up Valo?" Lea asked unsure.

"It's Flo." Flo replied in a nonchalant demeanor.

"Awe, sorry baby, can't really tell y'all apart," Lea responded in an apologetic voice. Lea who stood 5'2 with light brown eyes, nice small perky titties, and a nice small bubble booty was still very much beautiful at 34. The drugs haven't fully taken the best of her yet, honesty, if she wasn't so popular with her usage you'll never knew she smoked crack. She actually was a high commodity to the local hustler and dope boys, that's what made her a big spender. She had sponsors all over Miami, from dope boys to wealthy married men, known for some of the best and sloppiest head in Miami! Long story short she was a beast. Shit just went from sugar to shit and when she went from sniffing powder to smoking crack. Some people still couldn't believe she was a smoker, not Sasha's friend. Flo was happy he ran into her this morning.

"Just the person I was looking for," Flo stated extending his hand. Lea hesitated then reached her hand out. Flo drop the rock like substance in her hand.

"What's this?" she replied opening her hand noticing the small pink rock, she quickly closed her hand.

"What you think?" Flo replied inpatient.

"It's pink!?" she said with a surprise look on her face.

"I know." Flo replied with a smile of his own.

"Is it any good?" she asked skeptically.

"Yeah, it's the best shit in Miami." Flo answered confidently.

"And what do I have to do for this?" she flirted not sure if she wanted to trick off with her friend son.

"Nothing, just get the word out here," he said brushing her off and giving her his trap phone number. "Let muthafuckas know it's some new shit around that's better than all that shit y'all out here smoking… this shit called Pink drop."

"Okay, lil daddy, I will," she stated walking away seductively to the alley pulling out her glass pipe.

*'She doesn't waste no time…'* Flo thought continuing walking to the store. Opening the door to the neighborhood corner store he instantly felt refresh. He could feel the cool air from the air conditioner and it felt so good on his skin. Omar the store owner greeted him with a head nod. "What's up Omar?" Flo spoke. Omar was a small man at 5'7, 160lbs, bald head with a grey beard.

He was in his fifties. He'd been knowing the twins since they were just little kids stealing candy bars before school.

"Nothing man, how yo momma been?" Omar question curiously.

"She been good," Flo assured. "I'll tell her you asked about her next time she call."

"Make sure you do," Omar demanded.

"I will; let me get five back woods and these two orange juices." He paid for the items and left the store. Walking out the store he bumped directly into Lea almost dropping his bag. "Damn ma, watch where you going," Flo spat. She was also with two other crack heads.

"Hey, Flo, this is Rideout and Nefe." Lea introduced.

"We wanted to see about this new shit she says better than Baby'nem shit." Rideout spoke up interrupting them and avoiding the small talk. "You got sum mo testers?" Shit'd, he was ready to get high, he was tired of the bull shit dope he was wasting his money on.

"Man, how she makes it sound it's even better than Roach and Choppa'nem shit in Orange Mound projects too," Nefe interrupted.

"Oh, yeah? Here y'all go and here's the number, get the word out, we the new kings of Miami. These testers are on me," he boasted.

Pulling out her pipe Nefe put her shit right on her glass dick and sucked away like a pornstar. Holding it in and damn near coughed up a lung, "Oh, shit Rideout he not lying," Nefe admitted after she recovered. "I haven't tasted no shit this pure since the eighties." Following suit Rideout did the same thing and got the same reaction.

"Aye April, get ova hear this lil nigga got that Pink drop shit, it's like the eighties all over again," Rideout yell excitedly. 10 minutes later he was outta testers with a line full of crack heads following him back to his apartment. With a smile on his face he called Valo.

"Fuck taking you so long?" Valo picked up on the first ring.

"Man start bagging up, I got an army of hypes following me back to the building. You should see this shit mane, and they all want that Pink drop," he said seriously.

"Okay, bet," Valo replied.
*"What a morning…"* Flo thought smiling.

# Chapter (3)

"I ten a foe, $500?" Ondat boasted excitedly blowing on the dice.

"Bet!" Stevo replied dropping five big faces.

"You don't ten a foe to me too?" Flo challenge matching his enthusiasm.

"Drop that shit," Ondat replied smiling.

"I'm about to buy my bitch a Gucci purse off this nigga," Stevo laughed dapping Lil Prince. Lil Prince stood on the sideline with a big wad of money in his hand waiting to get in on the action. Between the five of them, including Valo, who was also standing on the sideline waiting on his turn to shoot the dice had to have like twenty-thousand-dollars on the concrete. The block was jam packed! It was bitches everywhere walking around in next to nothing trying to get the young hustlers' attention. By the way they were doing it, you would have never guessed that the crew was just dead broke and starving three weeks ago.

Funny how these were the same hoes who wouldn't give them the time of day with the exception of a few new faces. Thanks to Valo and Flo whip game, that Pink drop was taking over the neighborhood. Not to mention, that they had action coming from all over Miami to taste that Pink drop. Valo being the number guy came up with bagging up both kilos in all dimes. No matter how much money you were spending you had to buy whatever you wanted in dimes. It made sense due to the fact that they didn't have a plug to reup with yet, that was the only problem; plus, they only had about a quarter key left in dimes any way.

They were supposed to meet some guy Stevo knew, but Flo didn't want to just jump in bed with some outta towner's without doing the proper home work on them. Being that they had the best shit around the customers were always happy. Being the real niggas, the Twins were, they quickly put their day ones on. Stevo, Lil Prince, Ondat, Dee Dee, and OD was their day one niggas through it all, even though OD was locked up they made sure that they kept in touch with each other on a regular. He barely called knowing his guys were always up to no good, and knowing all his calls was being recorded he decided it was best to not call as often.

"I'm coming out!" Ondat announced shaking the dice. He threw the dice and one spinned a little then landed on a two, the other one landed on a three. He picked up the diced and repeated the process, but this time one dice landed on a three and the other one landed on a one. You heard oohhhs and ahhhhhs coming from random people in the crowd. "Y'all niggas sweet!" Ondat boasted picking up a portion of the money. Being that his point was ten he had to shoot again.

"Bet back!?" Flow challenge once again.

"Double or nothing," Stevo stated dropping a thousand.

"Bet!" Ondat answered smiling.

"He do it?" Lil Prince stated getting in on the action.

"Bet!" Valo spoke up dropping his money against Prince bet.

"Shake them muthafuckas," Flo replied trying to throw Ondat shot off.

"You want a shake go to Wendy's Or Burger King, they got all the shake you want!" Ondat stated causing Lil prince and a couple of locals to laugh. "Here these bitches come now…" Ondat stated shooting the dice and letting them fly. One dice bounced on the concrete and rolled on a five, the other dice spinned in a circular motion spinning on a two, but abruptly stopping and landing on another five.

"Point!" Ondat and Lil prince yelled almost at the same time.

"Ten, the muthafucking hard way!" Ondat bragged gathering his share of money.

"I'm done," Stevo replied looking at his phone. He was already hours late picking up his girl from work, resulting in her having to call an Uber once again. When it came to gambling, Stevo would lose all his money if push came to shove, he was more of an all or nothing type of nigga. He usually won though, but today Ondat was hot on the dice kicking ass and taking names.

"Me too." The rest of the gang started agreeing. Seeing the dice game was over the crowd start dispersing.

"Aye Valo, can I talk to you for a minute?" Tiffany his downstairs neighbor flirted. She was standing there watching the dice game. Valo looked at her in her pink booty shorts and white tank top and licked his lips.

"I'll be right back," he told the gang.

"Yeah, right," Lil Prince snickered.

At 23 years old and standing about 5'9, Tiffany was 150lbs all ass and hips, mostly ass; she had some small titties though. Light brown skin, big pouty lips and thick jet-black eye brows with dark brown eyes. She was definitely a bad bitch, ghetto fabulous bad. She even had a pink wig on that she paid about five-hundred-dollars for. It wasn't no secret though, Tiffany was a certified gold digger. If you didn't have nothing going on and if the outcome didn't equal income she wasn't fucking with you.

"What's the word ma?" Valo asked following Tiffany into the building. She looked back while walking up the stairs and caught him all in her ass, knowing that he was caught he smiled shyly trying to conceal his now hard dick.

"I want to show you something," Tiffany smiled deviously switching even harder knowing she had him in a trance. Entering the small apartment, she shared with her two sisters, Kiesha and Jade, she closed the door behind them.

"Where everybody at?" Valo questioned. Turning around and aggressively pushing him to the door she savagely began kissing and sucking on his neck. He began kissing her back. The sexual tension had been building up for months between the two. Dropping down to her knees she began undoing his pants and pulling out his already hard 9-inch-long thick dick, just the sight of it made her mouth water. Knowing he was the next nigga up, she planned on sucking the soul outta him. She believes if she can get him hooked she'll have unlimited access to his pockets.

Moaning, she began kissing and licking around the head of his dick making his already hard dick even harder. Using extra saliva, she began coating his dick with spit, slowly deep throating him.

"Damn ma, eat dat dick!" Valo moaned slowly fucking her face. Tiffany was a freak, and hearing Valo talk dirty only motivated her to go harder. Feeling him hit the back of her throat she began to relax her throat and let him have his way. Valo increased his pace and began fucking her face slightly faster causing her to gag a little resulting in slob running down the side of her mouth. She was playing with her pussy the whole time. Looking down at Tiffany on her knees with his thick hard pipe in her throat was enough for him to blow. He began to tense up and stood on his tippy toes grabbing the back of her head humping harder. Tiffany was loving every minute of it and her eyes began to water.

"UM, UN, UM, AWE SHIT, I'M ABOUT TO CUM MA," Valo moaned. Believing in finishing the job, Tiffany grabbed the back of his hips and began forcing him deeper in her throat. Valo began cumming down her throat and then pulling out while bussing the remaining of the cum all on her face and mouth. She began slapping his dick on her face. Seeing that he was still hard, she stood up and pulled her shorts down revealing her pretty pink shave cat. She bent over bussing it open for him, all that ass was enough to make Valo throb. Valo reached in his pocket and pulled out a condom. He knew fucking Tiffany was wrong due to the fact that he been fucking with her lil sister Jade since freshman year in high school.

True he had feelings for Jade, but Valo was a dog, he dogged her out most of the time. He felt that no matter what he did she wasn't going no were. He knew he was that nigga and with the new found fortune he had, you couldn't tell him shit. Don't get me wrong though, Jade was by far the prettiest sister outta the trio, but Tiffany was just as pretty with a lotta more ass. Tiffany grabbed the condom from Valo and put it in her mouth and skillfully began to put it on his dick with her mouth. Successfully, securing the condom on his dick she stood back up and bent over turning her head to the side and laying it flat on the table. Looking back at him with her ass in the air she batted her eyes.

"Fuck me," she seductively demanded.

Valo began walking up to her with his pants around his ankles and grabbed her ass cheeks. Being his first time actually grabbing them, he felt his temperature rise. Just as he was about to go in her wet pussy somebody began beating on the door.

"Tiffany unlock the door I gotta pee." She heard her lil sister say twisting the door knob. Valo and Tiffany panicked fumbling to put their clothes back on. Valo put the condom rapper back in his pocket leaving the condom on his dick. Kiesha began knocking harder. "Tiffany hurry up damn, why you got the damn door locked anyway?" Kiesha stated angrily bouncing left to right feeling like she was about to piss her pants.

"Here I come," Tiffany hollered.

"You good?" she asked Valo.

"Yeah, I'm straight," he replied nervously.

"We gone finish this," she said looking him in the eyes. Feeling like the coast was clear, Tiffany opened the door. Kiesha rushed pass Tiffany heading straight to the bath room but stopped dead in her track when she spotted Valo. Looking him up and down and seeing the bulge in his pants with the guilty look on his face, Kiesha smirked.

"What y'all in this bitch doing?" she asked amused.

"What?" Tiffany faked Offended, "Shit he came down here looking for Jade."

"Ummm humm," Kiesha replied sarcastically. "Jade and Choppa on the way up the stairs," she announced more like a warning then anything rushing into the bathroom. Hearing her lil sister and her boyfriend name brought her to reality. I mean she knew that they were on their way back, but she didn't think they would be back so soon. Walking through the door Choppa was also caught off guard by Valo presence. He didn't like nor trust the lil sneaky nigga, he felt Lil Prince was the only lil nigga out the clique he could see himself fucking with.

"Baby!" Tiffany exaggerated jumping in Choppa's arms. Choppa was mugging Valo as he hugged Tiffany and grabbing her by both her butt cheeks. He began tonguing her down marking his claim stunting on Valo. Choppa was wise to the looks Tiffany and Valo often shared and took pride in the fact that the lil nigga couldn't fuck with his bitch. Tiffany wouldn't have given a lil nigga like Valo the time of a day, so he thought. Let him tell it, Valo couldn't fuck with a picture of him and he didn't stand a chance with his bitch. Unbeknownst to him, Tiffany just had Valo whole dick in her throat not even twenty seconds ago, yup the same mouth Choppa was just tongue kissing.

It took everything in Valo power not to laugh, but he couldn't help the smirk that came across his face.

"Sum funny lil nigga?" Choppa asked in an aggressive tone. Not knowing that the joke was definitely on him.

"What I tell you about that lil nigga word?" Valo replied in an even tone. Sensing the animosity, Tiffany grabbed Choppa arm.

"Baby Valo just here waiting on Jade, speaking of Jade, where is she?"

"Here she come," Choppa replied never taking his eyes off Valo. Just as the stare contest was about to begin Jade walked through the door.

"Hey, Bae, I didn't know you were here," Jade stated rushing in his arms looking as lovely as ever. She was a dime. Being that she was mixed with black and white gave her that long hair, light skin, and light brown eyes that drove men crazy. Believe it or not, Valo was the only man she ever fucked. He popped her cherry freshman year of high school and she been stuck ever since.

"Hey, Bae," Valo replied actually feeling guilty now knowing that he let Tiffany give him head just minutes ago. "I came down here looking for you and sis…" he said referring to Tiffany, "told me that y'all was on the way back so, I waited on you," he stated confidently. "I bought you this…" he stated pulling out a jewelry box. Jade grabbed the box and looked around to all eyes on her. She opened the box and it was the most beautiful necklace that she'd ever saw, it was a heart with diamonds around it, and when you opened the heart it said 'Valo and Jade forever.'

"Oh, my God baby, it's so beautiful," she stated with tears in her eyes. She hugged him tight and kissed him. His phone rang and he looked at the caller ID noticing it was a jail call, then he answered.

"I gotta take this," he said abruptly rushing out of the door, "imma call you," he stated looking back at Jade.

"Okay, bae, love you," she replied.

"Okay, bro be safe out there," Tiffany replied sincerely.

"Okay, I will sis," Valo replied.

Watching the exchange between the two, Kiesha shook her head looking disgusted at her sister, whole time thinking bitches aren't shit…

# *Chapter (4)*

"**S**ay mane," Chase spoke in a southern drawl, "You say they beat the homie Jimbo with a hammer?" he asked curiously.

"Yeah, mane, they did the homie bad mane," replied Blac Vontay in between passing Chase the blunt of Jalatto kush they were smoking.

They were riding in the white on white G Wagon that Chase had recently bought under the table from one of his favorite dealer ships in Atlanta Georgia. Thanks to the late Jimbo, their plug from Miami who was recently killed, they were balling. Now, that he was gone they were running outta work and the duo started to feel it in their pockets. They needed a plug, and fast. Easier said than done though, trying to find a plug with the same or similar prices, and quality Jimbo was giving them, wasn't gone be an easy task.

"Damn mane, Jimbo was a good nigga, they didn't have to do the homie like that. What type of nigga beat a nigga to death with a hammer anyway?" Chase asked sympathetically. "A crazy muthafucka. You gotta be a crazy muthafucka to do sum shit like that," Chase stated answering his own question.

"It would have been way simpler if they would have just shot him, but don't even trip," Blac Vontay assured, "we're going to go down to Miami and get to the bottom of this shit. We can't let the homie die in vain like that though, plus, we need to find a muthafucking connect ASAP," Blac Vontay added.

"Remember, we gave that nigga that golden gun for his birthday?" Case asked.

"Yeah," Blac Vontay responded, "the nigga thought he was James Bond on his 007 shit. I'm sure gone miss that nigga though… we're going to have to go down there."

"What we supposed to do down there? We don't know shit about no damn Miami, we ATL shawty, all we know is these streets, the slums, the Six baby," Chase spoke passionately.

"That's the problem, we might as well expand," Blac Vontay stated. "King Lando'nem getting bigger, they got 4th Ward on lock and they shit already been just as pure as ours, how long do you think it's gone be before them fools start serving the Six shawty?" Blac Vontay spoke logically.

"The day they step foot in the Six that's the day them fools gone sign their fucking death warrant," Chase stated with hatred in his heart. "Plus, we don't know no muthafuckas out there in Miami," Chase reason. He heated the thought of leaving the 'A,' he knew the minute they left and word got out they were gone King Lando and his crew would take over the 'A' instantly.

"I know a nigga," Blac Vontay replied with a smile on his face. "My cousin Choppa, he's not that much of a hustler, but I'm positive he can show us who is who and the ins and outs, shit like that. He'd been there his whole life so I know he know who doing what, he might can even point us into the right direction of Jimbo's killer or maybe another plug."

"You sure?" Chase asked warming up to the idea. "When the last time you talked to that fool? And what about NeNe?" Chase asked referring to Blac Vontay baby momma.

"Mane dat gold digging ass bitch mane! Besides, what's it to you nigga?" he asked looking at Chase funny. "She'll be straight," he huffed, "I'm starting to hate that bitch, it's like she gotta GPS on my dick. It seems like every time I'm with a bitch she just magically pops up." Blac Vontay stated angrily, remembering the last few altercations she popped up on him with one of his many bitches.

"That's cause yo ass move sloppy," Chase stated laughing.

"Nawl mane, for real, I literally paid to get my car and shit swept for tracking devices and shit," Blac replied serious. Blac Vontay who stood 6'3 and 180lbs was black as tar, tall and lanky with a bald fade that kinda favored the rapper Lil Boosie.

Chase was about 5'10, brown skin with long dreadlocks with a soft voice. He was originally from Detroit. He was the only boy so he seems to get emotional a lot, a trait he picked up from his sisters. "A tracking device?" Chase laughed, "Man you know shawty not that damn smart mane."

"I don't know mane, it's like the bitch got a muthafucka spying on me or sum," Blac Vontay said seriously.

"You an old paranoid ass nigga," Chase laughed flicking the remaining of the blunt out the window, "but if she do got a muthafucka spying on you they ass dead meat," Chase said looking his best friend in his eyes.

Fuck friends, they were more like brothers. When Blac Vontay's pops died he lost it, if it wasn't for Chase being there every step of the way there's no telling where Blac Vontay would be. I am my brother's keeper and that's the mentality the duo had. Just then, Chase's phone rang and he didn't even bother to look at the caller ID, he picked up on the first ring.

"Hello?"

"Hey baby, what you doing…where you at?" A slurty voice asked. Tensing up, Chase cut the volume down on his phone with his left-hand real slick.

"I'm with the homie on our way to the waffle house about to get sum to eat."

"My pussy wet," she wined, "plus, I got something for you to eat right here," she moaned like she was playing in her pussy.

Hearing NeNe talk so nasty caused Chase's dick to begin to stiffen.

"What you on mane?" he asked getting turned on.

"Come and find out, you know where I'm at and take your garbage to the trash," NeNe stated seductively then hung up.

Chase was in deep, he knew he shouldn't be fucking NeNe, but he couldn't help it. He was hooked. She was thick, 5'3 130lbs, hazel green eyes, she looked black and Mexican, plus she was freak nasty being all about pussy. He just couldn't help himself even if she was his best friend baby momma.

**Boom, Boom, Boom, Boom, Boom, foc, foc, foc, foc, foc, foc, foc, tat tat tat tat**, gun shots roared in the air. The back of the G wagon window shattered, the bullet missing Chase's head by inches.

"Awe. shit it's a hit!" Chase served. Looking in the rearview mirror he spotted a black on black Nissan Maximum with black tints. He floored the gas running a red light barely avoiding hitting the back of a red pick-up truck.

**Boc, Boc, Boc, Boc, Boc, Boc, Boc, Boc**, Blac Vontay upped his 9mm he had tucked and began shooting through the broken glass causing the Nissan to swerve a little.

"Make a right mane and take this all the way down, then make a left, if they come we got they ass because it's a dead in," Blac Vontay stated ducking down in the passenger seat.

Grabbing the wheel Chase made a hard right almost causing the G wagon to tip over.

"Watch out, watch out!" Blac Vontay screamed noticing a young girl no older than five years old riding her bike in the street, but it was too late. The vehicle collided with the young girl and knocking her off her bike about ten feet in the air killing her instantly.

"Oh shit!" Chase yell speeding up.

"Damn bruh, pull over," Blac Vontay demanded.

"Hell, nawl mane!" He turned left and cut across a yard jumping into the next street.

"Pull over bruh, you hit a lil girl," Blac Vontay panicked.

"Hell, nawl mane, them white folks gone put me under the jail… fuck that lil girl!" Chase snapped checking his rear-view mirror cutting down another block.

"Slow this muthafucka down we lost them niggas bruh," Blac Vontay ordered noticing they wasn't being followed anymore. "Turn right," Blac Vontay demanded. Chase quickly turned right then made a quick left before Blac Vontay can even tell him. "Where you going mane?" Blac Vontay asked curiously.

"Don't NeNe stay on Ak'nem block?"

"Yeah, bruh," Blac Vontay replied in a daze. Following the familiar route Chase got there in record time. Pulling around the block into the alley Blac Vontay hopped out and opened the garage. Chase pulled in carefully pulling next to Blac Vontay Jaguar. Blac Vontay close the garage. "What the fuck mane, you hit a kid bruh!" Blac Vontay screamed screwing his face up.

"I know mane, you know I didn't do that shit on purpose," Chase stated offended. "I know mane, but we gotta lay low."

"Hell, yeah," Blac Vontay agreed. "We got muthafuckas shooting at us and shit, we don't even know who the fuck it was. I can bet you a million dollars that it was that nigga King Lando's people," Blac Vontay stated. "When I was bussing back, I could have sworn I saw that lil nigga Delyuntay laughing and pointing and shit. I'm sure it was his yellow ass and you know he not going to move without King Lando approval," Blac Vontay stated heated.

"Man, if we got that lil wild ass nigga Delyuntay on our ass we need to regroup, that lil nigga unpredictable, we gotta lay low we just killed a lil kid mane," Chase stated.

"We?" asked Blac Vontay bucking his eyes.

"You know what I mean mane," Chase stated lighting a blunt. "Shit'd, I guess that Miami trip don't sound too bad after all," Chase liking the idea even more now.

"Yeah, mane, imma call my cousin and set it up."

"Mane we can drive, we'll just split the drive time," Chase stated.

Just then, NeNe walked in the garage door catching the duo by surprise, both of the guys immediately aimed their guns pointing them at her almost blowing her shit back.

"Ahhhhh!" she screamed grabbing her chest. Taking a deep breath, they lowered they guns.

"Don't be sneaking up on us ma, we almost smoked yo ass mane," Chase stated.

"What the fuck y'all doing in my garage?" NeNe asked sassy, draped in a Gucci robe with her hand on her hip.

"We had a fucking shoot out and had to get low," Blac Vontay confessed.

"Awe hell nawl, y'all muthafuckas can get the fuck out, I got a son… yo son," she said pointing at Blac Vontay.

"Man kill all that noise," he replied nonchalant walking pass her heading into the house. "I gotta grabbed sum shit and we bout to hit the road." Walking pass her he told Chase hell be right back.

As soon as he was outta sight, Chase walked up to NeNe looking around making sure the close was clear and they began passionately kissing. Grabbing her big soft ass cheeks his dick hardens up instantly. Chase grabbed NeNe's neck and squeeze it,

"You my bitch," he told her spiting in her mouth. She swallowed his spit and moaned, that nasty shit turned her on. She was a pure freak, she didn't know the meaning of regular sex. Pushing her over the hood of Blac Vontay's Jaguar she turned around and Chase lifted her robe revealing that she didn't have nothing on under it. Swatting down Chase grabbed her booty cheeks and opened them. He then began kissing her ass cheeks and around her ass hole. Moaning, NeNe grabbed his head and looked down at him,

"Eat my ass Daddy," she demanded. Before she got the words all the way out her mouth Chase had his tongue in her ass hole licking it like his life depended on it. "Awe shit yeah Daddy, eat that ass," NeNe moaned.

Knowing his best friend could walk in at any minute only excited him even more. Chase stood up and pulled out his dick. NeNe looked back at his dick and shivered, he had to be at lease 9inches and thick, she could see the pre-cum dripping out his dick. Chase rubbed his dick around her ass hole, NeNe moaned and pushed back on his dick. Pushing slowly Chase began to enter NeNe's ass.

"Dammmn ma, this shit feels so good!" Chase moaned grinding slowly in and outta her ass.

"Awe shit daddy, fuck me…" NeNe moaned. Chase began to increase his pace, "harder, fuck my ass harder baby…" NeNe moan. Chase began to pound her ass hard.

"Oh, my God I'm cumming out my ass," NeNe screamed cumming all on his dick. Feeling her cumming on his dick was enough for Chase he began cumming all in her ass.

"Ahhhhh shit baby, daddy cumming in your ass," Chase moaned.

"Cum in mamma ass daddy…" NeNe moaned.

"Ahhhhh shit…" Chase said cumming. Drained, he slowly began slipping his dick outta NeNe's ass. "Clean daddy up baby," Chase demanded looking NeNe in her eyes. NeNe dropped down to her knees and began sucking the cum off his dick. Hearing the back door opening signaling Blac Vontay was on his way back, they quickly separate with Chase jumping in the passenger seat of the Jaguar. And NeNe wiping her face with her robe sleeve. Entering the garage Blac Vontay instantly sense something was wrong.

"Bitch, you think I'm stupid huh?" Blac Vontay barked.

"What?" NeNe asked heart dropping.

"Bitch you think I'm stupid?" he repeated. "I know what the fuck going on," he stated looking at Chase, Chase braced himself. "Bruh, this bitch thinks I'm slow or something, this bitch been going in my stash." Letting out a deep breath NeNe glanced at her baby daddy.

"Jr. needed some shit and I had to pay a few bills," she stated relieved he wasn't wise to the fact of what her and Chase just did.

"Whatever, I'm out I'll be back in like a week or two, don't fucking move this car and stay outta my shit!" he ordered hopping in the driver seat of his Jaguar. "I'll call you," he said pulling out the garage.

Whew that shit was close she thought excitedly making her pussy even wetter. They say the more you let a nigga know about you the more dangerous he become to you. Blac Vontay was about to find out the hard way.

# Chapter (5)

"You think we can trust this bitch bruh?" Flo asked in a skeptical voice.

"Momma said she knew her, but talking to her is our choice so she gotta be valid," Valo countered with confidence. "Besides, what other choice do we got bruh, she knows so much shit about us we done came too far to turn around now, plus we outta work."

"Yeah, we missing plenty bread," Flo agreed.

"You know they calling us the Dime Boys?" Valo asked with a smile on his face.

"Dime Boys?" Flo asked with a frown.

"Yeah, bruh," Valo said smiling.

"Fuck you smiling foe, you like that shit or sum?" Flo asked with a confused look.

"I'm just saying, that shit do have a ring to it. Name one set that got rich off dimming bricks up, plus we got a Dime Limit."

"Shit, why they don't call us Dime Limit then?" Flo asked amused.

"Shit'd, they do, they call us both," Valo smiled.

They were far from home, they were in the Virgin Islands, St. Thomas to be exact, they were laying on the beach just chilling.

"Man, bruh its hot as fuck out here," Flo stated fanning his self.

"Yeah, but it's some bad bitches out here though," Valo smiled checking out the honeys on the beach.

"I wonder why momma urged us to come here and meet up with this bitch?" Flo asked always suspicious about something.

"I don't know, but this bitch gotta be paid, you see the rooms she put us in? The first-class treatment and shit," Valo asked excited.

"Yeah, I do," he agreed.

"I wish the guys could see this shit, it doesn't feel right without the gang bruh."

"Stevo got you saying that gang shit too?" Flo asked irritated.

"Yeah, bruh, them niggas from Chi-Raq crazy, low key that shit be rubbing off on me."

"So now you think you from Chicago?" Flo asked picking Valo brain.

"Hell, nawl I'm Miami til I muthafucken die bruh, you know that, I just fuck with Chicago niggas they hard bruh, Lil Prince'nem be rubbing off on me with they're funny ass accents too," Valo replied.

"It's crazy how that one lick just changed our life, I mean just a month ago I couldn't do shit for Jade and now she can have whatever she like."

"Look bruh, I not trying to tell you how to run your shit, but fucking Tiffany isn't any good look," Flo stated.

Valo became agitated, "How you find out about that?" Valo asked.

"Just be cool, it's something about Tiffany and I don't trust her bruh. Fuck all that though, remember when we first met bruh'nem when they moved on the block?" Flo asked reminiscing.

"Yeah, bruh'nem was bout to jump our ass," Valo agreed.

"They wanted our bikes bad as fuck."

"Shit'd, if it wasn't for Rick Rick and OD they would have had our shit," Flo stated.

"Yeah, momma made us fight they ass head up, and once Stevo start getting in yo ass she made me jump in," Valo stated remembering the fight. "Man, them was the days and we clicked instantly after that though," Valo smiled.

"Them the guys fa life, shit'd, them the only brothers we got, shit'd we all we got," Flo spoke passionately.

While they were talking, two big ass Cuban niggas walked up to them.

"Veronica well see you now," the men spoke with a heavy Spanish accent.

"Bout time," Flo barked, "it's hot as fuck on this beach." Following behind the Spanish men they were led to the parking lot and into an all-black Range Rover. Feeling the cool air conditioner Valo sat back and relaxed. Flo stayed alert though, he didn't trust a muthafucken soul and he was slightly agitated that Valo was so relaxed.

"*Man, I wonder what the fuck this trip about,*" Flo thought, and continued... "*I know momma not gone lead us into no trap. This can't be her plug though, we've been asking her for that shit for about five years now, and all she kept saying was that isn't the life she wants for us. Maybe it's someone she knows, maybe it's about the lawyer? Yeah, that's what it is...*" he assured his self. "*It gotta be...*"

After about thirty minutes the car began to come to a stop.

"We here," the driver stated breaking the twins train of thoughts.

The three-level mansion was beautiful, it was surrounded by a big black steel gate while the house far off in the back. The drive way was long leading to a six-car garage. Once they entered the garage, they saw that it was full of luxury cars, the one catching Valo's attention the most was the pink Maybach Benz on 22" forgis. The license plates read Queena. Getting out the car they followed the Spanish guys inside the house. The sight took their breath away. The celling was high and the floor was marble. The stairs were off to the side and it led to the upper level of the home. The kitchen was beautiful and everything was new in the house. You can see through the patio out of the bay window. The pool in the back turned into a beach.

"These muthafuckas getting money bruh," Flo whispered amazed.

Just then, a beautiful Cuban woman began walking down the long stairs. She was about 5'7, 130lbs and thick in all the right places. Jet black hair, long eye lashes and she looked to be in her early thirties. She had the same eyes and thick lips like Sasha, the similarity took both, Valo and Flo off guard. Only difference was her boobs was much larger and they bounce with every seductive step she took down the stairs. Looking at the boys with a smile she noticed that both of them was staring at her boobs causing her to blush.

"Valo, Flo, nice to see chu guys," she stated not really knowing who was who.

"Nice to meet you to, Mrs. Veronica," they spoke almost at the same time.

"Its miss, I've never been married," she stated showing them her left hand, "these guys don't know what to do with this pussy these days, and call me Veronica." She spoke smiling. It was something about the twins that she liked already, their presence and lustful glares made her feel young again. The look of hunger and lust in their eyes intrigued her. The conversation she had with Sasha was a hard one.

"Sasha they're ready now," Veronica told her sister on the burner phone she just received. Sasha was asleep when the kitchen worker brought the cell phone under her breakfast tray.

"No, they are not Veronica, and we are not having this conversation right now." Sasha stated annoyed.

"Oh, yeah? What if I told you this..."

And for the next 30 minutes she updated Sasha on everything Valo and Flo have been up to. Sasha was impressed, surprise, and confused.

"Take care of my boys, you hear me sis? I'm counting on you," Sasha demanded. And here they were.

"You guys were much too young to remember me, but I'm your Aunt Veronica, Sasha's older sister," Veronica stated. "I first met you guys when you were maybe, five or six when Sasha brought you guys to Cuba to meet me; family."

A slight recognition flickered in the twin's eyes even though the details were blurry, they remember taking the trip.

"I never knew how she could tell you guys apart."

"I'm Valo," Valo announced extending his hand.

"And I'm Flo," Flo spoke up.

Ignoring the twins' hand, she pulled them in for a hug.

*"Damn she smells good,"* Valo thought hugging her extra tight. Pulling back, she looked Valo in the eyes and blushed again.

"It's an honor to be here and we appreciate the plane, and the first class and everything, but can you please tell us why you bought us all the way here to talk when you could have just said what needed to be said on the phone?" Flo asked curiously.

"You don't waste no time, do you?" she asked Flo caught off guard by his straight forwardness.

"We don't never use phones, when I need someone I come to them face to face. Would you guys like a tour of me home, something to drink, maybe"? Veronica asked in broken English walking seductively to the kitchen, unlike Sasha, Veronica was full Cuban. The twins' eyes were glued on her bubble shape ass as they began following her.

*"Damn she wearing that dress,"* Valo thought. She had on a red body-hugging Versace dress cut low to the chest of her double D's playing pick a boo under the garment. With 6-inch red bottom heels, long thick legs, and beautiful toes; her toe nails were also painted red, so was her finger nails. They followed her into the patio area were the pool was located.

"Have a seat gentleman," she gestures handing the twins' bottle waters and pointing to the patio deck were the seats were placed strategically in the shade overlooking the pool. The twins took the water and took a seat. Veronica took one of the seats opposite from them seductively crossing her thick thighs.

"I'm not gonna bull shit you guys, I've had my ears to the streets of Miami since my sister was apprehended by the Feds and I've never found a reason to sept foot back in Florida since then," Veronica stated. "You boys have made a little name for yourselves," she accused. "But there's one little problem," she continued.

"Yeah, what's that?" Flo asked sarcastically sensing the bullshit coming.

"Y'all have taken something that belonged to me and in result killed one of my best earners," she stated looking them in the eyes. Tensing and feeling like they walked into a trap, both twins reached for their gun, but came up empty, they couldn't bring no guns on the plane so they weren't armed. Amused, Veronica looked on and admired the fearless look in the boys' eyes. She was tired of Jimbo anyway, he was getting sloppy, she knew his days were numbered and she knew she needed new blood. Someone that was hungry, someone that was starving, someone that will get it by any means necessary; she needed hustlers and the twins looked promising.

At first, she put a hit out on Jimbo killers, but the surprise she got when she found out it was her nephews really intrigued her, she was even more amazed of what they did in the few weeks they had with the product. That was one of the main reasons for this meeting. The main reason she contacted Sasha.

"So, what, you bought us here to kill us or sum?" Valo asked clenching his jaw.

"If I wanted you dead you would have been dead the day you took from me," Veronica stated in a cocky voice. "You're here because I'm offering you an opportunity of a lifetime," she spoke louder with a smile on her face.

"What makes you think we need one?" Flo asked hostile.

"Like I've told you, I've had my ear to the street and I know everything, I know all about the 'Dime Limit,' you Dime Boys are running shit and I quite frankly, think it's genius," she stated with a smile. "The question is," she continued, "are you boys ready to take it to the next level?" she finished.

"What you talking?" Valo asked interested.

"My father was sad when Sasha went to jail, he loved Sasha with every bone in his body, but you two are not really blood so he won't hesitate to cut your throats and feed you to the sharks."

"And you saying this to say what?" Flo interrupted.

"I'm saying this because I'm offering you guys a deal of a life time, and if you fuck it up, you guys can end up dead," Veronica stated.

"Okay, what we talking?" Valo asked rubbing his hands together.

"To start," Veronica spoke, "ten kilos of pure Columbia Cocaine at let's say...twenty-thousand an apiece."

The twins were ready to do a backwards flip, but they knew to keep their poker face if they learned anything from the streets, it was to never let your right hand know what your left was doing.

"Well, I see it like this," Valo spoke, "in two to three month we'll be buying twenty keys from you, and six months from now we'll be buying any were from 30-50 kilos at a time, granted that it's the same shit ole boy had. So, I say we pay about thirteen a key and we can move them fast at that price."

Frowning, Veronica stood up, "What make you think I'll agree to that?"

"Because you know with or without you we going to find a plug and eventually become kings of Miami. Ain't no crew gone be fucking in our business. We plan on being bigger than the Cartel and we got killas just as deadly as Mecca was."

"And hungrier too," Flo added.

"You boys are crazy," Veronica stated impressed. "Okay, here's what I'll do, I'll do sixteen a key and if you progress to thirty or more we'll negotiate again, take it or leave it."

"Deal!" The twins said at the same time before she could even get the words outta her mouth, to be honest, they were happy with the eighteen a kilo, but Valo being the number guy just loved to negotiate. Veronica was prepared to give it them for ten thousand a kilo, but it all worked out for everybody. As if on que Veronica's daughter walked in. Both the twins' mouth dropped, she was in her bathing suite about to go for a swim unaware that it was company in the home.

"Queena, meet your cousins Valo and Flo." "Hi," she blushed in a nervous chuckle, she never seen men so beautiful and identically beautiful at that. She felt that familiar tingle down below. They looked street and being sheltered she was always intrigued about guys like them. She instantly notices both of the boys checking her out. At 5'5 with light brown eyes like Veronica's, she was Cuban and black like Sasha. Her hair came down to her ass. She had beautiful tan skin, perky breast and a nice petite body with a solid bubble booty. She also had a slight accent, she actually looked just like Veronica but darker with smaller boobs and braces.

"Nice to meet you guys, I'm Queena."

"What's up ma, I'm Flo," Flo spoke up extending his hand looking her in the eyes. Shaking both boys' hands, she began to blush again. Seeing the exchange between them Veronica spoke up.

"I was just discussing business with your 'cousins'." She said cousins with a lil extra on it, somewhat jealous of her daughter taking all the attention away from her.

"Sorry to interrupt," Queena stated. She looked over her shoulder and spoke, "I hope to get to know you both better, cousins," she winked diving in the pool. Clearing her throat Veronica spoke.

"I'll have your shipment ready and delivered in about a week from today with the total coming out to $160,000, half now half later, any problems?" Veronica asked all business.

"No, not at all," the twins agreed confident that they can move the ten kilos.

"Okay, fair enough," Veronica agreed standing up. "You boys enjoy yourselves, your plane will be ready in the am. The package will be delivered to you guys a week from now, I will send a contact to pick you guys up and take you to the dealer ship I own in South Beach. The contact will then give you keys to a car with instructions on how to work the safe compartments, once done you will put the money in the same compartment and my contact will come to pick up the car. It will be a different car every time and a different place every other time, deal?" She asked looking at the brothers.

"Deal!" They both agreed at the same time.

Laughing Veronica asked, "So twins really do that?"

"What?" Valo asked.

"Finish each other sentences?" she asked.

"Sometimes." They both answered at the same time. They all got a good laugh outta that one.

Leaving the mansion, the twins knew their prayers was answer and they could only thank two people, God and Sasha. Sasha continued to be there for them even from in jail.

*"Damn we plugged..."* Valo thought.

*"Thank you, momma, imma get you home this what I've been waiting for..."* Flo thought hopping in the back of the Range Rover heading back to his hotel.

# Chapter (6)

The room was silent, the only thing that could be heard was the air conditioner and fan that was sitting on the floor by the living room table. Standing up, Valo paced back and forth in front of his gang. Ondat, Stevo, Lil Prince, Rick Rick, Flo, and DeeDee, was all listening intensely.

Dee Dee was a tom boy, she was originally from New Orleans but stayed in Florida half her life. She was the only girl in the clique and probably the quickest one to pop off, she got busy with them pistols. She was often mistaken for a boy but truth be told, under all them baggy clothes she was beautiful, nice body and cute face. No one in the gang ever saw her dressed like a girl. She was that, pretty brown skin, long hair that came down the middle of her back, she often wore it in single braids that looked like dreads with a hat on.

Rick Rick was also a part of the clique, him and Flo seemed to be fighting over who can catch the most bodies because they were both racking them up this year. Only person was missing was OD, and he was truly being missed. Looking everyone in the eyes Valo spoke.

"How long I've been knowing y'all?" he asked to no one in particular.

"Shit'd, since we were shorties," Dee Dee answered jokingly.

"To damn long," Stevo commented with a smirk of his own.

"What's this meeting about bruh, who gotta die?" Rick Rick asked with venom in his voice. Everybody looked at him like, what he asked? The room erupted in laughter.

"Man, if you don't cool yo trigger happy ass down," Ondat laughed.

"Nawl bruh, that isn't why we here," Flo spoke up.

"Awe," Rick Rick replied disappointed.

"So, what's up?" Lil Prince asked.

"Y'all know we have the hood on lock with the Dime Limit and shit, right?" Valo asking pausing.

"Yeah, we killing them bruh," Stevo agreed.

"We got the hood on lock, but that's not enough… y'all ready to lock down the fucking city?"

"Hell, yeah," Lil prince yelled, he was the youngest. He was about 18, also brown skin with boyish features, low fade and kinda look like the Chicago rapper, G Herbo.

"Shit'd, how we gone do that and we outta work?" Dee Dee asked curiously. "Plus, it's a lotta competition in Miami," she continued.

"Fuck the competition, any muthafucka in our way can get it." Rick Rick snapped.

Valo looked at them and held his finger up, "Wait one minute." Valo went to his small room to retrieve the duffel bag he got from Veronica's contact earlier. Walking back to the table he began to dump the contents on the table cockily; speechless, everyone looked on in amazement. The ten beautifully wrapped bricks of cocaine fell from the bag.

"Them real bricks bruh?" Stevo asked scratching his dreads.

"Yeah, my boy, pure Columbia Coke." Flo spoke up

"Where y'all get this shit from?" Ondat asked thinking they hit another lick and left him hanging again. Looking at the bricks like they were a pot of gold the gang was impressed.

"Let me touch one of these muthafuckas bruh," Dee Dee asked picking up one of the bricks being all extra and shit. "I never held a brick in my life," she stated in awe, "this shit looks good my boy," she screamed.

"Where y'all get this shit from?" Stevo asked excitedly.

"I'll share the details later," Valo replied, "what we need to do is get down to business. I'm ready to sow these muthafucken streets up," Valo spoke passionately.

"What we gone do about the Hot Boyz, you know they got shit on lock right now?" DeeDee asked

"Fuck the Hot Boyz they bleed just like us," Flo retorted with a mud on his face. "I want y'all to listen because after today there isn't no turning back, we not blood brothers, we getting shit out the mud so that make us mud-brothers, we're Kings," Flo continued looking everybody in the eyes. "And Queens," he stated smiling looking at Dee Dee.

"Niggas fuck you," she laughs.

"On some real shit, we plugged now." Valo interrupted, "We gotta pipe line coming straight from Cuba. Them joints going for like $32-$33 bans out here, imma front each of y'all these muthafuckas for $21,000 apiece." He felt since he was plugged and taking the most risk, and getting them for $16,000 allowing him and Flo to split the $5,000.

"Depending on what blocks we take over going to determine how much y'all make," Flo added.

"This the plan, any block y'all got your eyes on we gone put pressure on that bitch and push muthafuckas out," Valo stated.

"Why sell thangs when we made over a $100,000 a brick when we sold them bitches in dimes?" Ondat stated.

"That shit take too long and it eventually gone bring us a lotta heat. How long did it take us to make that $100 racks?" Flo asked.

"About a little over a month," Dee Dee boasted.

"Exactly," Valo stated, "and that was with all of us bussing our ass at the same time. We split that money in seven ways, we only had two books." He continued referring to the bricks of cocaine as books.

"We could have made more, but you refused to stretch it," Lil Prince complained.

"Good he didn't, that shit y'all whipped up had the block on fire, especially with that pink die in it, that shit was genius," Rick Rick smiled.

"Why stretch it when you selling dimes? Shit gone take forever to get off," Stevo said.

"Right, make sense," Lil Prince added.

"Look, this here…" Valo stated pointing around the apartment, "is going to be the headquarters. I've arranged it with the landlord to give us the two vacant apartments upstairs, we'll have the whole building, with the exception of Tiffany'nem shit down stairs. We're gonna start here tomorrow, cooking and getting this shit on the streets. First, get the word out that if you buy two dimes you get one free. That goes for every first fifth and fifteenth of the month."

"I know a few niggas who buy ounces, I can run through a brick or two in ounces of hard, like this..." Stevo spoke up snapping his fingers for emphasis.

"Okay, check this out, what I can do, I'll front whoever want a brick to do their own thang in the future or however many y'all can handle, but as of now, if anybody want one y'all can just give me eleven now and eleven later."

"That's $22,000!" Ondat spoke catching the thousand dollars increase.

"Yeah, that extra thousand is for the whip game," Valo said.

"Okay, bet, let's get this money," Stevo shouted all smiles doing the numbers in his head. He was glad his mud-brothers volunteered to whip it up, he wanted that same quality... that Pink drop.

The next day came and they made good on their promise, the twins fronted Stevo, Ondat, and Dee Dee all a brick apiece with the three of them giving up eleven thousand apiece. Rick Rick and Lil Prince decided to play the block, they felt why use your own money when you can make money off someone else money! It made sense because they were a big part of the muscle out of the gang. They were promised three thousand a day no matter how good or bad the block did. At the time it seemed like a good idea plus, they loved the hood, they had all the hoes around all the time and they loved to be in the middle of the action.

The twins couldn't believe how the ordeal was turning out, they spent the first night whipping the dope putting the pink dye in it. They cooked four bricks and bagged them in ounces, they were supposed to come out with 144 ounces altogether, but the dope was so pure they came out with 216 ounces turning four bricks into six. It was way purer than the shit they got off Jimbo. Due to the drought, they were able to charge whatever they wanted, people were literary charging $1500-$1700 an ounce, but they decided to keep it real and charge a $1000 an ounce. They felt why not? They had the plug, why not show the hood some love, not just they hood but every hood in Miami.

They wanted to corner the market. Word spreads fast when you got the best dope with the cheapest prices, before you knew it they had niggas coming from all over Miami. They even had niggas coming from other parts of Florida. The hoods loved the mud-brothers and they were becoming local celebrities among the underworld. This one nigga Pimping Paul came through. He was riding in a clean candy red Cadillac truck. The block was jam packed as usual.

"What's up pimping, you straight?"

"Flo, my main man what's going on?" Pimping Paul asked in his best pimp voice.

"Same shit different day," Flo responded. "What's up with you, and what brings you to this neck of the woods?" Flo asked.

"Mane I was wondering if you had some of the Pink drop in the powder form, you know I gotta keep the hoez fed."

*"Yeah, right,"* Flo thought, *"nigga you know this shit for you..."*

"I do, but you know that's gone cost ya," Flo stated.

"Ain't no shortage on this shit young blood, my money long as the interstate. I wish y'all ass was shooting dice today, I'll tear a hole in y'all ass today."

"Now you know you not fucking with none of the gang," Flo laughed.

They made their transaction and everything went smooth as butter. A month went by and as promised they nearly double what they were buying from Veronica. The twins were a firm believer in you couldn't eat were you shit so, the twins rented them a condo on the north side of Miami beach. Valo also brought a spot for him and Jade, she was so happy.

"Baby it's so beautiful and big," Jade gushed looking around the beautiful home Valo cashed out on.

"You like it ma?" he asked her.

"I love it baby!" Jade responded kissing Valo on the lips.

Valo grabbed her hand, "Come and look at how big this garage is ma," Valo demanded. Valo walked in front of Jade and opened the door, Jade walked in and her jaws dropped.

"Baby you didn't?" Jade cried. They'd always talk about they dream car since they were in high school as freshmen, she'd always tell Valo that her dream car was a pink Benz coupe. He'd always tell her that one day he would get her one. He just didn't know how, but he pulled it off and Jade was the happiest woman in the world. They made love right there inside the Benz.

The days were like a dream come true. Every day was toss-up. The gang was unpredictable, they were having the time of their life, but with more money comes more problems. This particular morning Flo woke up feeling like a new man. Valo was already gone, he knew early bird got the worm, he ate, showered, and got dressed. Both Valo and Flo had master bed rooms with a full bath room attached. Flo's phone rang and he picked up noticing the familiar number.

"Hello," he answered.

"What's up boo?" Kiesha flirted.

"What's up ma?" Flo replied.

"Shit'd, trying to see you." That was her code for she needed some more work. She saw the way the Mudbrothers was getting money and immediately asked the twins to put her on. Being she stayed in the same building and was a known booster she had that hustler's mentality already, and Flo felt why not? She was giving five-hundred-dollars a day to bag up the dope, do the dishes, and watch out for the cops. She was also able to buy a zip of hard for a thousand and sell it on the block in dimes; she would run through a zip a day some days, she was definitely eating.

Tiffany was also a part of the action, even though she was scoring for Choppa, she middle manned him. They served her nine ounces for nine thousand every three days which she served it to Choppa for $12,000 making $3,000 in the middle so, she too was making a thousand a day. Choppa would do his thang and call Tiffany when he needed to reup, everybody was happy. He could have probably easily called one of the Mudbrothers, but his pride refuses to let him shop with the lil niggas. He actually hated them for no reason, he hated the way they were cornering the market and taking over.

"Where you at ma?" Flo asked her.

"I'm up top, how long until you get here?" she questioned knowing how long he could take sometimes.

"Give me an hour," he replied rolling a blunt.

"Okay, I'm here," she sighted knowing he might be longer then he said.

Pulling up on the block Flo scanned the block and smiled at the dice game Lil Prince'nem had going on, he notices how packed it was so business was good! He was in his red 750 Li BMW fully loaded and he was fresher than a virgin pussy. He had on all white Gucci sneakers, white Gucci shorts with the green and red Gucci trimming, all white Gucci collar shirt with the green and red Gucci trimming around the arms and collar. He had his dreads freshly done in two barrels to the back. Walking up to the dice game he heard Lil Prince talking shit as usual.

"Imma hit this bitch, it's gone come tray tray," Lil Prince taunted. Shaking the dice and throwing them twice, he blew on them on the third try and sure enough the dice came tray tray. "I need a fader not a friend…" Lil Prince boasted while picking up the money.

"Bet five-thousand?" An unfamiliar voice challenged.

Pausing and looking up, Prince noticed two niggas he never seen before, clutching his gun Lil Prince stood up. "Who the fuck is y'all?" Prince asked.

Dropping the stack of money on the concrete Mula looked over the crowd, "I'm Mula," he spoke in an arrogant tone like he was king or some shit.

"Name doesn't ring no bell to me gangsta, who you supposed to be?" DeeDee asked.

"And do you know where you at?" Lil Prince asked harshly.

"Mula?" Flo spoke up, announcing his presence. "That name doesn't ring a bell to me either," he stepped up mugging the duo.

"You must be one of the twins?" Mula asked skeptically.

"Yeah, in fact I am," Flo responded with a smirk. Everybody was on the block except Valo, Stevo, and Rick Rick. Dee Dee sensing trouble walked off between the houses next to the building, Ondat stood on the side of Lil Prince as the crowd started dispersing.

Mula smiled looking at Flo, "I come in peace baby," he stated in a southern drawl.

"Fuck you want then?" Ondat stated picking up Mula's money and putting it in his pocket. Seeing the murderous looks in the young teens eyes he instantly regretted coming to the block without his gang.

"Speak yo peace," Flo stated amused.

"I'm here on behalf of the Hot Boyz," Mula stated.

"And?" Flo asked.

Looking around Mula noticed that the dyke chick was missing, *"Where the fuck that bitch go…"* he thought. "Since y'all opened up with that Pink drop we haven't been able to eat," he stated defiantly.

"So, what y'all want to join the team or sum?" Ondat asked with an attitude.

"Nawl my boy, we'll like for y'all to shut shit down or only cop y'all shit from us," Mula stated seriously.

"Shut our shit down or cop our shit from y'all?" Lil Prince repeated with a chuckle.

"Or what?" Ondat asked.

"My people not going to be happy," Mula stated a lil braver.

"Awe yeah?" Prince asked.

"Yeah," the Mula guy spoke up.

"Okay, this what we gone do," Flo stated digging in his back pocket, "y'all got a number?" Flo asked as if he was digging in his back pocket for a pen.

"Yeah, we do," Mula stated relief evident in his tone.

Pulling his hand out his pocket Flo upped his baby 9mm., he did it so quick, even his own team was surprised. "Fuck y'all think this is?" He asked pointing the gun at the duo. Mula's guy took off and tried to run through the cut, but was stopped in his tracks and hauled back at gun point by DeeDee, who was in the cut watching how everything was playing out.

"Fuck y'all the message boys or sum? Y'all know who the fuck we are?" Dee Dee yelled. "We got this shit out the mud and y'all want to take it?" **Wack-** she smacked him with the butt of her gun. "Bitch niggas strip," she continued.

**Wack- Wack-** Flo starting beating Mula with his gun and the next thing you know they started stomping the duo.

"Fuck the Hot Boyz…" Dee Dee screamed jumping on Mula's head with her two feet. They robbed the duo for all their money, Dee Dee took they clothes and made them walk home bloody and naked. "Tell yo boss that, bitch nigga," she stated after kicking Mula in the ass. The gang fell out laughing, but little did they know they shit was about to get very ugly.

# Chapter (7)
## - Stevo -

"Look my nigga, you already owe me five-hundred off the last shit and now you wanna owe me another five on this one?" I asked Biggs scrunching up my face.

"Look, Stevo my nigga," Biggs responded in a deep southern drawl, "What I'm saying is that, I have the five I owe you, but imma need you to give me a foe and a baby for 4g's, and I owe you five-hundred when I make this play. Matter fact, imma make it seven-hundred for the inconvenience, gangsta."

"Now, that's what the fuck I'm talking about my nigga," I said shaking Biggs's hand.

Biggs was a big ass nigga, he was like 6'7 310lbs, a straight killa though, a big Rick Ross looking ass nigga. I had love for him though because he was solid. He was just released from the joint doing a four-year bid for serving an undercover, but he kept it solid and I fucked with him the long way. We hit a few licks together before and I knew Biggs was a real dude plus, on some gangsta shit, he was just one call away. Actually, he was the cousin of my side bitch Jasmine and that's how we met.

Handing him the brown paper bag, Biggs took a peek in it,

"This that Pink drop, right?" He asked.

"You already know my boy," I replied with my signature smile. Usually, Biggs wouldn't buy work already cooked, but the way that Pink drop had his line ringing he was like, fuck it, he knew he couldn't lose.

Locking the door behind me, I flopped down on the sofa, we were conducting business at my main bitch Tokyo's house. Tokyo was my ride or die bitch, she was a part time stripper on the weekends, mainly so we can rob niggas. She also did home care on weekdays. She was a bad bitch, Asian and black, about 5'5 with a fat ass and chinky eyes with light peanut butter skin. She was always the main attraction at the clubs she worked at, she attracted all the ballers. That's how we got the drop on most of the licks, once she gets a hold to a nigga, for some reason they'll tell her anything. She made hoes insecure without even trying.

Just as I started to relax, Tokyo came out the bed room in some boy shorts and a wife beater, *"damn, my bitch bad…"* I couldn't help but think.

"About time that nigga left, with his big ass," she wined sitting in my lap. She was in the bed room waiting for Biggs to leave because she didn't have any clothes on. "You counted that money bae?" she asked me looking at the money in my hand. She had them hazel green eyes that looked in a nigga soul. See, that's why I loved my bitch she stayed on point, besides OD, she was like my best friend and she don't trust a fucking soul; and she'll pop that thang in a heartbeat.

"Nawl ma, I haven't counted that shit, that's my dude." I replied slightly irritated.

"Give it to me I'll count it!" she insisted. I gave her the money and she began counting it.

I grabbed the remote and put ESPN on. Just as the highlights started to play my phone rang, I picked up without looking at it.

"Yooo," the familiar voice greeted me that instantly brought a big kodak smile to my face. It was my nigga OD, I knew this nigga voice from anywhere. My boy was locked up on a drug charge, but since I've been getting money I was able to buy him a cell phone off the plug he had inside that bitch. This nigga always had a trick up his sleeve and you can bet on that.

"What's the word my boy?" I matched his enthusiasm.

"Shit'd, cooling, just waiting on my moment," he replied referring to getting out of jail. "I got that money too, good looking my boy," he continued.

"Yeah, everybody gave me a hundred to give you so, shit'd, I had Tokyo send it off for me," I replied.

"That's what's up," he replied. "Tell the guys I said I'd appreciate it, what's up with them hoes though, my boy?" OD asked in a player way.

Tokyo smacked her lips, "You know I'm a one-woman man," I said looking at her.

"Don't get fucked up OD," Tokyo screamed into the phone playfully. We were all close, OD actually was the one who introduced me to her about six years ago, they were friends first and they went to the same school together when we all stayed in

Chicago. I usually don't do that best friend shit because I'm a firm believer in nobody being closer to your bitch then you, but I trusted them and they were truly friends.

"You know I'm just testing yo game sis," he responded shyly through the phone. He really didn't know she was listening and he forgot Stevo had a habit of putting him on speaker phone and shit.

"What's this shit I hear y'all got going on with the Hot Boyz though?" OD asked getting straight to the point. I knew when he called me off this phone it was sum gang shit, he usually wanted to keep these types of convos off the record. What I was wondering though, was how the fuck he knew about that shit so fast? They say muthafuckas in jail find out everything first, so, I shouldn't be too surprised.

"Shit, Dee Dee wild ass stripped Mula and one of his flunkeys and made they ass walk home naked," I stated nonchalantly. Tokyo starting laughing.

"What'd?" she said with her hand over her month. Tokyo knew Mula and she knew his crew, they were always showing up to clubs where she worked making it rain and acting all tough and shit; so, the image of Mula walking home naked cracked her up. OD starting laughing too, he had this funny ass laugh that was contiguous, and before you knew it we all were laughing at the Hot Boyz expense.

"Why she do that shit?" OD asked confused, but still laughing.

"Flo say them fuck niggas came ova there talking about they not eating and we need to close down shop or cop our shit from them, them niggas lucky I wasn't there," I replied getting myself all worked up and shit. "Gang'nem stomped they muthafucken ears together," I smiled.

"You know that fuck nigga Baby gone try to make a move to save face, so y'all stay on defense," OD stated wisely.

"I hope he do so we can smash that ass," I replied passionately. "I wanna take over they muthafucking block, it's time we expand."

Baby was the leader of the Hot Boyz and he was a beast in the streets, he had shit on lock for a while until we caught that plug now the tables was turning and it was time we take all the way over.

A wise man always told me, why want a house when you can have a block? Why want a boat when you can have a yacht?

"I gotta go my boy, they about to do count, but stay on point and don't let y'all guards down. Dodat wrote me too, he says he get out the hole next week and he gone call. He also said he got that money too and sends his love," OD continued.

Dodat was Ondat lil brother, he was always doing shit and saying he didn't do dat or he really would do dat to a nigga. Every time a body would drop back in Chicago the police would come looking for him to ask him did he do dat so the name just stuck with him. Ondat was always on bull shit, you could just tell by the look in his eyes when he was on dat bull shit, that's how he got his name.

"Okay, bet, tell lil bro to hit me," I replied.

"Okay, love," OD said.

"Love my nigga," I replied.

"Love bro…" Tokyo screamed into the phone, "awe yeah, Yoku asked about you too," Tokyo stated in a hurry. She'd forgot, Yoku was her big sister, she was about 22 years old and Tokyo was 21.

"Yeah?" OD responded excitedly, "What's her number?" OD asked and she gave him the number. "Love gang, good looking out, tell her imma call her," he said before hanging up.

"I miss that nigga," I said getting sad all of a sudden.

"Me too," Tokyo replied. Together they were a gang. "Awe bae, I got the drop on that flexing nigga, he from ATL," Tokyo smiled lighting up the mode. "I've been on his ass like promised," she continued.

That shit definitely got my attention. See, me and my bitch ate in all avenues, don't get me wrong, I'm a bona fide hustler, but I was a jack boy by heart. I guess the saying is true, old habits die hard.

"So, what's to him?" I asked her.

"I don't know yet, but he definitely be flexing buying out the bar and shit, if you ask me, it's like he trying to draw attention to himself," she replied.

"Okay, ma look, keep a close eye on that nigga, he might become a victim, or he might become a potential customer, it depends on what's more beneficial," I replied.

"But of course," she replied with a sexy ass smile. "But in the meantime," she said grabbing my dick, "where were we before yo fat ass homie interrupted us...."

Two days later the block was full as usual. Rick Rick was sitting on the hood of his Audi talking to sum thick dark skin chick. Dee Dee was laughing and joking with Lil Prince.

"So, you mean to tell me you didn't use no condom gang?" she asked laughing in a confused voice.

"I can't say I didn't, and I can't say I did, man gang, that bitch must have put sum in my drink cause the next thing you know I was gutting the bitch out."

"You wilding yo," she replied, "look, here comes yo lil mans." Dee Dee said turning to face Lil Zay.

"What's up big homie?" Zay screamed excitedly walking up and shaking both Dee Dee and Lil Prince hand.

"What's up lil homie?"

"Nun man, just got outta summer school. I hate that bitch ass school though."

"Man, what I tell you about cussing?" Lil Prince asked in a serious tone.

"My bad big homie, but you always told me to speak my mind and that's how I feel. I'm a man, and a man says what he means and means what he says," Lil Zay stated.

Dee Dee smiled, she vividly remembers Lil Prince telling Lil Zay them exact words. Truth be told, Lil Zay was far from a man, he was only nine years old in fourth grade, but he was from the block and he mimicked everything Lil Prince did. At first Lil Prince found his behavior slightly irritating and annoying, but eventually he warmed up and took a liking to the lil homie.

"What you know about being a man lil homie?" Lil Prince taunted.

"I know that if a man doesn't work then a man doesn't eat," he replied pulling out a small bank roll. "See, y'all not the only ones getting money," he stunted with his fifty sum odd dollars, all singles with a five on top.

"Damn, lil man, you a drug dealer now?" Lil Prince asked getting heated. That's definitely not the road he saw for his lil mans.

"See, you gotta expand yo mind big homie, it's a million ways out here to get money other than the block," he smiled quoting Lil Prince. Lil Prince stood there beaming, he knew that Lil Zay was different and that's why he always dropped knowledge on him.

"So, what did you do lil nigga to get, a good report card or sum?" Dee Dee asked.

"Nawl, nothing like that," Lil Zay replied reaching into his book bag pulling out a bunch of candy bars. "I sell these at school, gotta help my momma pay the bills," he smiled, "y'all wanna buy one? There only a dollar apiece, but if y'all both shop I'll give them to y'all 2 for a dollar and fifty cents," he bargains.

Pulling out a big wad of money Lil Prince peeled off a hundred-dollar bill, "Give me one." Looking at the big face Lil Zay frowned, he didn't want to miss out on a sell so he had to think quick.

"Big homie I can't change that, I don't have enough, but give me five minutes and I'll run to the store for you for free and get you some change. Get you some juice or something, it's kinda hot out here," he smiled.

"Don't worried about it, keep the change," Lil Prince stated.

"Give me one too," Dee Dee replied also pulling out a hundred-dollar bill. They respected Lil Zay's hustle and was happy to see him do some positive to improve his situation, his momma had him young, but she did what she could.

"Thanks," he uttered excitedly, he was beyond grateful.

"Don't worry lil man, keep up the good work and keep yo hustle honest," Lil Prince encouraged. Thinking about the other sells he had lined up he started zipping up his book bag.

"I gotta go, I promised Omar, (the corner store owner) that I'll help him sweep up plus, he told me he was gone give me more candy bars for a discounted price."

"No problem lil homie, handle yo shit..." they told him giving him dap.

"Okay, stay dangerous," Lil Zay told them smiling mimicking Ondat. "He gone be big bruh," Dee Dee stated.

"Yeah, he a real one," Lil Prince agreed.

Just then, a dark color SUV rounded the corner with heavy tints noticing. The unfamiliar car instantly put Lil Zay on point, he stood there and watched it, he was half way to the corner store when he noticed one of the back windows of the SUV down, he saw the barrel of a gun.

"It's a hit!" He screamed warning Lil Prince'nem. Seconds later gun fire erupted. You heard at least seven different guns being fired.

"Don't let that muthafucka make it off the block," Dee Dee screamed as all returned fire kneeling behind a car.

"Damn," Rick Rick said ducking barely dodging a bullet flying pass his head. The thick dark-skinned chick Rick Rick was talking to felt it was safe to make a run for it, she tried to dash across the street and was caught like a deer in the head lights. She was hit multiple times with hot slugs, one bullet took off half her skull, she died before she hit the pavement. Speeding pass, the SUV made a brake for it smashing off leaving the block, all you could hear was burning rubber. Outta ammo, the gang regroup coming from behind the cars.

"What the fuck? Niggas think its sweet, we gone show they ass, y'all good?" Yelled Lil prince heated. Rolling from under a car Lil Zay was up dusting himself off. He was a few cars down so he still had to walk up to the gang.

"You saved our life lil homie," Lil Prince yell. They were all walking towards Lil Zay, they could hear police sirens in the distance. Just then, the same SUV spent the block one more time, Lil Prince heart dropped.

"Nooo..." he screamed, but it was too late. About ten bullets ripped through Lil Zay undeveloped body killing him dead. All you could hear was machine guns firing. All the gang was able to do was take cover because they were fresh outta ammo. So that's what they did. They could hear the police getting closer.

"Shit, I'm hit bruh," Dee Dee screamed holding her right shoulder.

"Shit!" Rick Rick curse. Hearing no more gun shots they felt it was safe to come from cover. They all rushed to Dee Dee's truck noticing that Lil Prince was missing, they looked up and saw him picking Lil Zay up. They all hopped in the truck speeding to the hospital.

"Damn, lil bruh hold on…" Lil Prince pleaded holding Lil Zay in his arms. Pulling up to the hospital reckless Lil Prince rushed in. "I need help, he's been shot!" Seeing all the blood the doctors rushed to take the boy outta his arms.

"Are you hit sir?"

"No, I'm not. Here, take this number and call his mother," Lil Prince stated giving the young doctor the scrapped piece of paper and rushing out.

# Chapter (8)

*I can't believe these stupid muthafuckas killed a lil boy. I gave them one fucking job to do and that was to hit them Dime Limit niggas, but nah, these muthafuckas went and did some wild-wild west shit. To make shit worse, they didn't even get the muthafuckas they were supposed to get. I swear I'm getting too old for this shit, then they kill a bitch too, yeah, shits about to be hot as fuck.*

That's all I could think while lying in the bed at the Four Seasons Hotel. It was about 8:30am and I couldn't sleep for shit after I had received the news about 3 hours ago. Turning over in the bed I had to admire the big booty stallion that was snoring lightly next to me. Honestly, I didn't know her name, I couldn't even remember if I asked her for it. One thing I did remember was how good her pussy and head was, and how much coke we shoved up our nose. Feeling like I needed a wake and bake, I reached over the night stand next to the bed and snorted a line. I instantly felt the blood rush to my head. I quickly took a shower, brushed my teeth, and got dressed.

Once I was done, I threw five-hundred dollars on the bed and crept out the hotel leaving the sleeping beauty sleep. Hoping in my Cadillac Truck I instantly called my right-hand man Mula. Mula picked up on the second ring.

"Baby, my nigga, I was just about to call you."

"Where you at bruh?" I asked him.

"I'm at the hide away."

"Don't move I'm on my way."

"Okay, bet, I'm here."

20 minutes later I was pulling into the westside condo. This was our hide away, only a selected few people knew about this spot. Walking in the house Mula greeted me at the door.

"You look like money B," Mula joked.

"Had a good night," I smiled. Baby was about 6'1, brown skin, low Cesar haircut, a baby face with a mouth full of platinum teeth; he was in his early forties, 41 to be exact.

Mula was about 6'2, tall and lanky with long dreads with gold tips, he also had a mouth full of diamonds and platinum, he was 33.

Walking in the luxury home he went into the bar area and was stopped dead in his tracks by what was playing on the TV.

{In other news today, there was a fatal shooting that left two dead on the west side of Dade county today. One in which we believe is a 19 year old unidentified female and one small child who we believe that was young as nine years old, both fatally shot and killed. The woman was pronounced dead on the scene and the lil boy was rush to the hospital where he later died at the hospital in results to his injuries. The details are sketchy right now, and the police are not releasing names at the moment, but there are no suspects in custody.}

Just then, the news reporter spotted both detectives, Detective Sarson who was African American, about 36 years old, light brown skin, tall athletic build, long brown hair with little blond streaks in it with a nice round bubble butt with grey eyes. She was known by the local drugs dealers as cat eyes. She made Detective about seven years ago and became partners with Detective Hollywood, she was a hell of detective.

Detective Hollywood was actually his last name, but it seemed like he took his last name to his head because of how flamboyant he dressed. He was a white man and racist as they come, a tall bald guy with patches of grey hair on the beard. He had a thang for putting young black men behind bars.

{"Detective, you care to make a comment on these shooting?"} Dress to impress and always up for publicity Detective Hollywood jumped right into the camera.

{"Well, we don't have any leads as of right now, but we're working around the clock to make sure we bring whoever did this to justice. We have reason to believe that this was a gang related incident, but what troubles us more is how much these nig... I mean people, are unwilling to cooperate in this community. It makes this case extremely more difficult and harder to crack. So, if there's anyone out there that saw anything please feel free to call the crime Stopper Hotline thank you."}

He finished walking out of the camera view.

{"Well, that would be all, I'm Nicole Jacobs, reporting live from Fox 5 News crew."}

"Man, what the fuck happened?" Baby asked making a sour face.

"Man, me and the lil guys went to handle that shit you asked us to do, and shit got outta hand" Mula stated.

"What you mean got outta hand my boi?"

"Shit got ugly B, it's like them niggas was waiting for us or sum, we most defiantly underestimated them lil niggas. We had to spin the block and everything, they even had a bitch out there shooting. But that isn't all B." Mula continued, "Word on the streets is that, them Sasha Boyz that got shit shook up like it is."

*"Sasha..."* B thought rubbing his chin. "Man, why the fuck does that name ring a bell to me?"

They were now sitting in the living room on the plush sectional lighting up a blunt, Mula took a big pull and blew the smoke in the air.

"Name ring a bell yet?" he asked.

"Nawl man, I'm over here trying to wreck my fucking brain, name sound familiar though."

"Sasha, Diewoo plug. The bitch that got snatch up by the feds and kept it solid, they say she was the baddest bitch to ever walk Miami."

"What?" B asked in an astonished tone.

Sasha was their plugs plug! Everybody knew about Sasha, she was a legend in Miami, people still talked about her to this day. She only fucked with a hand full of niggas and they supplied the whole city. The only female to single handedly run the city, she had shit on lock. She was their big homie Diewoo plug and he had them eating, but when the feds grabbed Sasha it's like he disappeared off the face of earth. Shit haven't been the same since.

"You know what, Sasha did have two bad ass lil twins," Baby acknowledge.

"Well, shit'd, word on the street is that they the ones who running shit on that block."

"Who you getting this info from?" Baby asked.

"You remember crack head Rideout?"

"Yeah, he been around for a while, he uses to be the man until he got hooked on that glass dick," Baby responded.

"Yeah, but he still reliable for information, he always in them streets," Mula stated.

*"Damn..."* B thought, make sense, who else can have some shit that pure with prices that cheap if anything, we gotta get these lil niggas on our team so we can get that plug or we gotta dismantle they ass. This bull shit we've been getting for the last six months not selling no more, now I know the reason why. The ringing of B's iPhone interrupted his thoughts. Looking at the phone and noticing it was one of his workers he instantly picked up the phone.

"Speak on it," Baby demanded slightly irritated.

"Boss don't come to the block whatever you do," Lil Rody said in a panicked voice.

"What you mean don't come to the block, what the fucks going on?" Baby barked angrily.

"Man, muthafuckas done came through and kicked the spot in and robbed and kilt everybody. Lil Man, Cam, Jay-R, and Rah Rah all gone man."

Baby heart dropped. "What the fuck you mean all gone?"

"They dead B," Lil Rody replied with tears in his eyes. "Muthafuckas came through like the A-Team and I'm lucky to be alive. Cam sent me to get some blunt raps and once I made it back to the block and went in the house, it was like a blood bath in that bitch! Man, it was bad, I wasn't gone but 10-15 minutes. That isn't all big homie," he continued. "They hit the spot on the south side too, wiped everybody out and blew up the house, didn't nobody survive that shit. My lil bitch on the block just called me and put me on game, mane the police out here a thousand deep bruh, theses niggas playing for keeps mane."

Baby was in disbelief. *"How the fuck can this shit happen..."* he thought.

Meanwhile, 15 minutes earlier on the South side of town Rick Rick, Ondat, and Stevo was sitting in the block on a Black Tahoe truck watching the block, everybody had on a mask. Each and every last one of them had Draco. They were here to send a message. Lil Prince, Valo, and Flo was sitting in the same model Truck on the next block waiting on the signal. The reason for the set up was just in case someone ran out the back door and thought they was gone get away. The caper where they killed Cam, Jay-R, Rah Rah, and Lil Man went down smooth, that was about

25 minutes ago… them boys didn't stand a chance. They used AK-47s for that mission, now they were headed to another trap house of Baby's'. They felt it was best to catch them now because they would least expect it.

Killing the men came easy to the young killas and they were just getting started. They were out for blood! Killing Lil Zay brought something different out of the youngsters. Avenging his death was all they wanted to do. Seeing the crack head coming outta the house was they que.

"Okay…" the crack head started. "It's one dude at the door, he seems like he got a gun, but I couldn't really tell, it was another dude that was sitting on the sofa, I saw a girl in there too. Oh, yeah, they never use the front door only the back."

"Okay, look, this is what I need you to do," Rick Rick spoke up giving her another twenty-dollar bill. "I need you to get them to open that door again and we'll take it from there."

"No disrespect to you, but we don't know you. We only know Lil Prince, we only here to do what he need us to do because he takes care of us," Tiny stated. Rick Rick frowned.

"It's cool shorty, handle that for my mans and imma really take care of y'all."

"I'm cool on that part," April spoke, "I did my part can I get my stuff and go?" April asks with her hand out. She had a good sense of what was going on and she didn't want no part of that.

Lil Prince gave her five dimes and she walked off. He had a feeling he shouldn't have let her walk off but dismissed it. All he could think about was Lil Zay.

The house was set up were you had to walk to the back to buy anything, they never used the front door which was new news to them. So, Stevo called the gang and updated them on the change of plans. This made it easier for the gang though, because there were a few people on the front of the block. Ondat was driving, he pulled to the back alley checking his surrounding until they felt the close was clear. Sneaking up to the back door they stood next to the crack head and watched her work her magic. She knocked on the door.

"Who is it?" a boyish voice boomed.

"It's me, Tiny."

59

"Awe, you came right back huh, I told big homie my whip game was proper," he boasted from the other side of the door unlocking it. Opening the door, the boy didn't even see it coming, Stevo grabbed the young boy by his shirt and slammed him to the floor.

"Man, what the fuck?" The boy spat in a surprised tone.

"Man, you know who spot you robbing? This baby shit!"

"Fuck baby," Stevo replied smacking the boy with his Draco.

"Shit man," the boy cried.

"Who all in this bitch?"

"Man, it's a house full, like 6-7 people," the boy exaggerated, "this the spot man, trust me you not going to make it out that bitch alive."

Just then, Lil Prince, Valo, and Flo arrived.

"What's the hold up?" Flo asked ready to spill some blood.

"He says it's like 6-7 people in that bitch."

"Don't matter let's roll," Rick Rick stated.

Entering the house, they could hear the music playing. You had to walk in the hallway to get to the other door that led to the house. Cracking the door, they saw four man at the table playing dominoes. Stevo who had the gun to the boy head and shoved him to the door.

"You first Joe."

Opening the door, the boy tried to be slick and rush through the door and warn the others. He pushed Stevo and tried to make a run for it, what a mistake it was. Stevo let off the Draco, the bullets hit the boy in the back and the back of his head. He then turned his gun on the crack head hitting her twice in the face. This caught the attention of the guys sitting at the table.

One guy, a chubby kid went for his gun but was chopped down by Lil Prince's Draco. That triggered the whole gang to let off their guns, it sounded like ground zero in that bitch. The dudes at the table died playing dominoes. They all rushed into the house splitting in twos, Valo and Flo, Lil Prince and Stevo, and Rick Rick and Ondat.

"Jack pot!" Lil Prince yelled walking into the room with a table full of money and drugs, and started bagging everything up. They quickly maneuvered throughout the house. Hearing more gun shots, they all rushed to where the sound was coming from. Walking in a back room Ondat was standing over a man that looked all too familiar to the gang.

"Isn't this the muthafucka that shot up the hood and kilt our people?" ONDAT smirked.

"Yeah, same tattoos, small world huh," Stevo replied.

"Who else was in dat car with you?" Flo asked.

"Please, God help me…" the man pleaded with bullets all in his upper body. "God please, help me…" the man gasp.

"Breath nigga, God help those who help them self," Ondat smirked. Then the whole gang emptied the remaining of the clips in him, well over a hundred shots.

"Let's get the fuck outta here!" Valo stated grabbing the bag full of drugs and money. They took off, but not before Rick Rick turned all the gas on the stove and setting the beds on fire… now we out he smiled.

Pulling out the alley and making a right, before they could even make it to the lights they heard a big boom. It wasn't no secret where that sound came from, all Rick Rick could do was smile. Stevo face timed Dee Dee who was at home recovering from getting shot in her shoulder.

"Watch the news bruh,"

"I saw it already," she smiled.

"Nawl, keep watching," he replied before hanging up.

"I'm hungry, stop at that pizza place by the block," Ondat stated.

"Bet," Stevo replied.

30 minutes later they were pulling into the Pizza Palace drive through.

"Welcome to the Pizza Palace how can I help you?" Some sexy dark skin chick asked. Licking his lips Stevo jumped in Mack daddy mode, after buying the food he got the girl number and promised to call later.

How they were carrying on, you would have never guessed that they were responsible for the 10 murders that occurred within the last hour. Little did they know this was just the beginning.

## *Chapter (9)*
## *- Chase -*

**M**an, I can't lie, coming to Miami wasn't a bad move after all. Even though we been cooped up in these hotels for the past week, I have to admit, Blac Vontay finally came through with this one. I've been fucking different hoes every day, bad bitches to! These hoes different then our Atlanta bitches, they wild and they love a nigga accent. Especially, this lil bitch Tokyo, this lil stripper chick that I've been after, I mean the bitch playing hard to get, but I'm most definitely gone get me a shot of that pretty pussy shawty. We suppose to meet Blac Vontay's cousin Choppa today. About fucking time, because we've been down here for about a week and we still haven't met up with this nigga yet.

He supposes to be the plug, or know the plug or sum shit like that. I don't know, something just sounds a lil fishy about his ass, but we'll cross that bridge when we get there. Blac Vontay can be weak sometimes, a lil naive. He can't even see through NeNe bullshit. Part of me feel bad for fucking my home boy's baby momma, but shit'd, I feel like this, if a bitch go she go. I know deep down he still love that bitch, and I've been kinda foul for telling her his every move but shit'd, she'd threatened to cut me off with the pussy and nawl, I can't have no shit like that, no bullshit. I have never met a freaky Mexican and black bitch like NeNe, she my personal porn star. I got plans for that bitch...

Chase thoughts was interrupted by the sound of knocking on the hotel room door. Grabbing his guns off the bed his 'twin bitches' as he like to call them, he tucked them in his waist and went to answer the door, he knew it could only be one person. Opening the door, he was greeted by Blac Vontay with a bag of food. Blac Vontay was a loyal nigga and he loved his homie Chase, he would and have laid his life on the line for his homie. But only if he knew that love wasn't the same.

"Bring yo ass on, we gotta meet my cousin in about an hour and we got a thirty-minute drive, let's make it shawty. Here, I grabbed you some food, I know yo ass haven't ate yet," Blac Vontay stated handing me the bag of breakfast food.

"My nigga," I stated.

"Mane, you been watching the news bruh?" Blac Vontay asked?

"Watching the news? Fuck would I be watching the news for, I'm just hoping we don't make the news fucking with these niggas down here," I replied.

"Don't sleep on these niggas down here mane, shit been going down out here, they say about ten muthafuckas got killed in an hour span last night."

"Damn…" That shit got my attention. "What, it's some type of war going on or sum?"

"Shit'd, I don't know, but they saying the victims appear to all know each other on the news and shit."

"That's fucked up, but that's why I keep my bitches with me," I replied patting my waist.

We walked to the luxury Range Rover we rented from the airport. We really didn't want nobody to know what we drove and I don't know about bruh, but I was definitely looking for a come up. I was definitely on my backdoor shit. But we did have the Jaguar in the cut just in case.

Pulling up to the address Blac Vontay gave us, I was surprised at how low key the block was. There weren't that many people on the block and our car blended in perfectly with the other cars.

"Follow my lead," Blac Vontay advised me.

I don't know who the fuck he thought he was talking to though, I don't follow suit, pussy ass nigga. That's what I wanted to say, but I played my part, I was looking at the bigger picture. I walked behind him at a nice distance eyes on alert, I have to be on point at all times, I done fucked way too many niggas up. To be aware is to be alive. Before we made it to the door some bad ass bitch opened it up. *Damn this bitch nice…* I thought.

"Y'all here for Choppa?" she asked welcoming us in at the same time.

"Yeah, Choppa my cousin shawty."

"Shawty? Y'all some ole country ass niggas, I know who you are though, I saw pictures of you before," she stated looking at Blac Vontay.

"Who is your friend?" Tiffany asked him looking me in my eyes.

Now I know bitches, been around them all my life so, I know for sure this bitch was giving me that look. This bitch was speaking hoe volumes that only boss players like me understand.

"I'm C shawty."

"Nice to meet you C..." she flirted.

"Like wise ma." This nigga Choppa must have felt me about to take his bitch because as soon as I was about to put my Mack down this nigga walk in.

"Cuzzo, what's popping mane?" Blac Vontay asked walking up embracing his cousin in a brotherly hug.

"Shit my nigga, trying to get this cake."

"I feel you on that," Blac Vontay agreed, "this my partner C that I've been telling you about."

"Yeah?" Choppa asked.

I peeped the nigga sizing me up, but I played it cool. I extending my hand and jumped right into mode, I didn't make it all these years by being a fool. "What's up big homie, I heard a lot about you." That instantly softened him up, sometimes you gotta play the lil homie role to get a person to let they guard down. 48 Laws of Power shit. He shook my hand.

"I've heard a lot about you too, you a young wild ass nigga," he stated. "I heard you don't mind bussing yo gun either," he stated.

"Shit'd, it be like that sometimes," I replied.

"Look, you family, any friend of my lil cousin is a friend of mines. Anything you want its yours while your here with me," he stated.

'*Good...*' I thought looking at his bitch, I was really smiling on the inside. *Yeah, I gotta finish reading that book, it taught me some shit,* I thought.

He walked us to the kitchen where he had another bitch in the kitchen cooking dope in a thong and she was a bad bitch too.

Choppa was doing his thang, he done came a long way from them nine ounces he was getting from Tiffany every three days, now he was getting three whole bricks every three days and shit was moving fast. He was selling ounces for $1300. It was safe to say them DIME BOYZ had the best dope for the cheapest prices in the city and them muthafucking ounces was moving like hot cakes. He paid thirty-thousand for a brick untouched, but when he cooked it up he turned 36 zips to 54 zips, and sold them for thirteen-hundred apiece pulling in about seventy-thousand every three days. He would middle man the other two bricks. Tiffany was really getting them for twenty-eight-thousand a brick from Valo, but she got her cut off top and she was stacking. There was a pile of money on the table.

My trigger finger started inching. I was ready to take sum shit, the wheels started spinning in my head, what Blac Vontay didn't know was that I was fucked up! Broke as fuck. I can't lie, I have a habit of tricking off with bitches and splurging at the clubs. All I had was about five g's to my name so, I was definitely on my taker shit.

"So, what's been good cuzzo?" Blac asked.

"Shit'd, this money, you know how we rocking," Choppa boasted.

"That's what I'm talking about, what's the numbers on them thangs?" Blac Vontay asked.

"Shit'd, you know how the game go, it depends on how many you getting, shit fucked up right now so that real raw shit going for about 35-36," he lied.

"Damn cuz, that shit high as fuck, me and bruh trying to get about four of them bitches, two apiece to start. I know yo people can do better than that, we do better than that back home," Blac Vontay stated.

"Okay, imma make a few calls, in the meantime roll this shit up and let's catch up on sum shit…"

On the ride back to the hotel I laid my head back in the plush seats of the Range Rover and collected my thoughts. Being around Choppa and them for a few hours taught me some valuable information about him, most important thing to me was that, that nigga wasn't the plug. Couldn't be. He most definitely was connected to somebody though, his line was rocking so hard, his shit had to be good. Once back at the hotel we both went to our separate rooms. Two hours later I got a knock on my door, smiling sleepily I got up and answered it.

"Right on time," I told her. I could smell her perfume blowing with the wind while she was standing in the door way, only thing that was different from the last time I saw her was she had her clothes on. She now wore some daisy dukes and a belly shirt.

"You gone just stare at me or are you going to invite me in?" she asked.

Stepping to the side I invited her in. I couldn't take my eyes off this bitch. Tiffany was a bad bitch, she could have been a bad ass stripper shit'd, she probably was, I mean I didn't even know the bitch from Adam or Eve, yet this bitch was at my door. She was bold too, I loved me an aggressive woman. At first, I thought it was some type of trick when she gave me her number behind Choppa's back, but she did that shit so slick I knew she was different, I knew I had to keep my eyes on her because this bitch was sneaky.

"So, what's up shawty? You just skipped out on your man and shit, and now you here with me… what am I missing?"

"Nigga knock it off, you know what it is, besides, I love me a sneaky ass nigga," she smiled.

"What makes you think I'm a sneaky ass nigga shawty?" I faked offended.

"Nigga please, I'm the backdoor Queen, I'm always plotting my way to the top, the eyes don't lie and I'm always open to making some money when the opportunity presents itself," she stated with a smiled

"Okay, and you saying this to say what?" I asked her licking my lips.

"How I see it is like this, y'all niggas need a plug and I might can make that happen for a better price then what that nigga Choppa giving y'all."

Her motive was to have Choppa and Blac Vontay buying weight from her, that way she can middle man them right under Choppa nose.

"What's in it for you?"

"What do you mean what's in it for me?" she asked making a face.

"I know you not doing all this back-dooring shit for nothing," I stated looking her sexy ass in the eyes.

"Is that really the question? Does it really matter?" she asked me.

"Not really ma," I replied. *I like this bitch* I thought.

"How much money are you working with?" she asked me. For some reason I decided to keep it real with this bitch. Something told me she was different. "Shawty, I'm not gone lie, I'm fucked up and only have like five g's to my name."

"Five g's?" she repeated. "Y'all niggas were talking like y'all wanted a few thangs apiece!"

"See, bruh been saving, but I been fucking off, splurging and shit."

"Perfect!" She responded to my surprise.

"How determine are you to get them bricks?" she asked me.

"Determined," I replied.

She smiled, "I got a few niggas lined up I wanna hit, they are just in the way, dumb muthafuckas. I mean loaded, they with cash though. I needed a few new faces to make shit happen and what's newer then an out of towner?" She smiled.

"What I gotta do?" I asked her.

"You ready to get shiesty?" she asked me.

"How can I not?" I smiled quoting my favorite rapper Future...

The night air was nice and warm with a slightly nice breeze, the block was deserted and it was about 2am. I had been sitting down the block watching the house for about 45 minutes. So far what I've learned was that it was just a dude and a chick in the house. The traffic had just stopped, from the Intel I had, the shop was supposed to close at 2am every night, and that's when the count up start. Sneaking down the block I eased my way to the front door. I stood there for a minute listening to the door and I couldn't hear shit, but lucky for me I knew the lay out. It was now or never for me.

Checking my twin bitches to take them off safety, I pulled my mask down, I was ready, do or die. I stood back and kicked the door with all my might, it came crashing down then I rushed in the house and went straight to the kitchen. Sitting at the kitchen table getting his dick suck was no other then Choppa, caught with his pants down, literary. On the table was about four piles of money and a money counter. I recognized the woman giving him head, it was the woman from earlier that was here with Tiffany. Choppa tried reaching for his gun that was on the table, but I had the ups on him.

"Don't even think about it playboy, hands were I can see them," I yelled in a disguised voice.

"Don't shoot man," Choppa pleaded.

I made him and the bitch get on the floor and tied them both up. I grabbed all the money off the table and I started searching the house, I found another small pile of money, two guns, and a half of brick of powder to go with the money that was on the table. I was so excited I could hardly think. Putting everything in two pillowcases I rushed to the door. To my surprise Choppa was gone. Rushing out the door I went desperately looking for him. It didn't take long for me to find him because he was hopping down the street still tied up. I caught up with him and kicked him in the back. He went flying to the ground. I could hear him moaning and pleading through the tape.

I knew he was my homie cousin, but shit'd, it was just business for me, besides, this nigga almost got away. Before I knew it, I pumped three shots into his chess. *Bitch ass nigga,* I thought. I quickly rushed back to the whip and got outta there. I safely navigated my way back to the hotel. The whole ordeal took about two hours. Once back in the room I dumped all the contents from the lick on the bed. The half of key of coke and two guns was put into my duffel bag. I was surprised at how much money this nigga had. In total, I counted $177,000 dollars. I put twenty-thousand dollars to the side. Man, this shit felt good. I haven't had this much money at one time in a while.

I started to call NeNe. I just couldn't wait to spoil her. I was lowkey in love with her toxic ass, damn I was in love with my best friend baby momma. I then reached for my phone and sent a text to Tiffany and said, "Done."

"Okay, on my way," she quickly replied.

Thirty minutes later Tiffany was knocking at my door. I let her in, she was dressed more comfortable this time with a big ass purse. I handed her the twenty g's I promised her.

She smiled, "Okay, I expect everything went well?" she asked. "Yeah, something like that." She gave me a look. "What?" I asked her.

"What did you do?"

"Shit'd, I had to kill Choppa."

"Wait what, why?" she asked hysterical.

"Nigga tried to go for the gun and it was either him or me," I lied.

"Fuck, fuck, fuck…" she stated hitting the table. She felt bad for Choppa, I mean he was supposed to be her boyfriend, but thinking about the twenty-thousand in her purse she smiled, "Niggas die every day B," she joked heartless. "Okay, look, on Choppa you did good, and I gotta few more licks lined up, but imma need a bigger cut. I let you get the bigger cut so you can get on your feet, but next time we do sixty forty your way."

"Cool," I replied. I'm loving her cut throat style. Turning to leave I jumped up and grabbed her arm. "Why don't you stay for a while?"

She looked at me, "Boy please, I know you don't think you was getting any pussy," she yanked her arm away.

"You just killed my man." I smiled at her… isn't this about a bitch.

"No more bodies," she yelled over her shoulder on her way out the door.

# Chapter (10)
## - Valo -

I woke up to the sound of Jade yelling in my ear.

"Really, Ja'Valo really?" Barely woke, I shifted to my side agitated. First thing I noticed was my cell phone in her hand. I instantly cursed myself. I came home late last night. I was a little tipsy when I came in, I don't remember much after that. I had a lock on my phone so I knew she couldn't get in my shit. I looked at her, "What's with all the yelling ma?"

"Don't fucking ma me, who the fuck is this bitch?" She asks throwing my phone in my face. I looked at my phone in disbelief. It was a picture that Dee Dee sent me of one of her bitches' friend in her birthday suite. The caption read… "Pussy good isn't it?"

The first thing that came to my mind was how the fuck she got in my phone? The second thing that came to my mind was, how the fuck I was going to get out of this shit, and how much did she actually see? Next, thing I know I was getting hit in the face with a pillow.

"Answer my fucking question Ja'Valo."

I just looked at her dumbfounded, to be honest, I didn't hear a thing she said because I was too deep in my thoughts. She stormed away from me and went to the closet as if she was about to pack her shit. We were at the crib I'd brought for the both of us. At first, I just stood there waiting to see how shit was gone play out, then I saw the tears and my heat just broke into pieces. Truth be told, I love Jade. I mean, yeah, I fucked off on her a little bit, I knew I was wrong, but she was the only woman I ever loved, the only woman besides Sasha that I ever cared for. I trusted her with my life… she was my ride or die. We were high school sweet hearts, she didn't leave me when I was broke, she been here since the beginning.

I was just addicted to pussy. I can still hear Stevo voice now.

"You got a good one their bro, she the one, she loyal, don't let her get away!"

I walked over to her, I tried to grab her but she yanked away. I grabbed her arm more firmly. "Baby, it's just a picture, I don't even know her, the picture was sent to my phone," I spat out truthfully.

She looked me in the eyes, "did you fuck her?"

"Hell, nawl baby," I replied. "I don't even know her, I never even seen her in person."

"Well, why is her picture in your phone?" She asked with tears in her eyes.

"I forgot that it was in there, I just disregarded it when it came through." I hugged her, "baby I'm sorry."

She cried in my chest, "what's wrong with me, why is this happening to me? I give you all of me, I'm here for you all the time, I don't even look at other niggas, but yet you still put me through so much shit Ja'Valo. I just want to be happy and love you forever," she cried.

I hugged her even tighter. I knew I had to change because Jade was my heart. We stood there a minute and I let her cry until she let it all out. I started kissing her neck, "imma be better ma." I then began sucking on her neck, I knew that was her spot. I felt her loosing up. I firmly grabbed her face and softly began kissing her. Kissing her made my dick hard as a steel pipe. She grabbed my dick through my boxer briefs feeling my hard, warm flesh in her hand and it caused her pussy to moist. She moaned in my mouth still holding my dick, she stopped kissing me and pulled her head back then smacked the shit outta me still holding my dick.

I instantly grabbed her neck, she tried to smack me again but I caught her hand. She began jagging my dick as I squeezed her neck a little harder. I went to grab her hand so I can pen it behind her back so she won't swing again, but to my surprise it was under her robe. My dick jerked. I love my bitch, she was a freaky freak, my product, and she was really into rough sex. She took her fingers from outta her pussy and shove them in my mouth. I hungrily sucked them. She took her hand out of my mouth and put them back in her pussy, all the while she was still jagging my dick. She then dropped to her knees. She pulled my briefs all the way down, I stepped all the way out of them.

She grabbed my dick and began giving it wet kisses. She then spat on it making it slippery. She knew how I liked my dick sucked, I taught her very well. She started sucking on the head, she got into a good rhythm and before I knew it she had my whole dick in the back of her throat. Now, one thing I knew about Jade was that she liked her throat fucked. She got off to that freaky shit. Not to be the one to disappoint I began fucking her face. She just looked at me with slob dripping down her face just letting me have my way, she had her fingers buried in her pussy the whole time. I almost busted a nut, I had to control myself. I tried to moved her head because I didn't want to cum, but she slapped my hands away giving me the green light. I grabbed the back of her head and long stroked her mouth.

"I'm cumming ma, what the fuck, all my God…" I moaned cumming down her throat. I recovered quickly and picked her up off her knees and we began kissing again. She loves when I kiss her after she'd sucked my dick, she says that it's taboo. I laid her down on the bed and she snatched off her nightgown. I dived in her pussy face first.

"Oh, my God baby…" she moaned. I licked along her pussy lips. I opened her lips and began nibbling on her clit, I felt her clit hardening up so I stuck a finger in her pussy and began finger fucking her while still licking her clit. "Yes, daddy eat that pussy."

I took my fingers out her wet pussy and stuck my whole tongue in it. She grabbed my head and began fucking my face thrusting her pelvis in a circular motion. As I was tongue fucking her, I was rubbing her clit really fast at the same time. She let go of my head and I began licking her clit really fast and finger fucking her even faster with two fingers. She grabbed my head again,

"I'm cumming daddy."

She began to convulse, when she started shaking and shit I knew my tongue game was the shit. She came all in my mouth and I swallowed every drop of her sweet nectar. I kissed her because she liked the taste of her pussy on my lips. I put her legs on my shoulders and eased into her pussy. She took a deep breath, after all these years she still wasn't accustomed to my size. Man, her shit felt like a tight wet glove, like her pussy was made for me. She slapped me again. I went deeper in her pussy and slapped her back. She came instantly. I was fucking her hard, long stroking her fast.

"I love you Ja'Valo baby, punish me, beat this pussy up, teach me baby, teach me…"

Just the thought of her going in my phone cause me to unconsciously grip her throat tighter.

"I'm cumming on you dick daddy," she screamed. That was enough for me,

"Ahhhhh shit ma, I'm cumming in your pussy…" I came so hard and violently that I collapsed on top of her. We just laid there for a minute.

"Bae, get off of me I'm running outta oxygen," she joked. I got off her. We just laid there staring at each other. Make up sex was the best. She laid her head on my chest.

"So, I asked randomly, how did you get in my phone?"

"I used your finger print while you were sleep dummy," she smiled.

I chuckled, "I didn't think of that," I admitted.

"You gotta stay on point boo," she stated kissing my chest.

"I love you though bae, and I'm sorry for having that picture in my phone."

She playfully punched me in the side, "You better not let that shit happen again," she said in a playful, yet serious voice. I grabbed her and we started play fighting.

The ringing of my cell phone interrupted our moment. I located my phone on the floor next to the bed. Seeing it was Flo facetiming me I picked up.

"What's up mane?"

"What's up bro?" I replied.

"Shit'd, this money mane, you still in the bed?" he asked.

"Sum like that, Jade had me tied up," I laughed looking at her.

"What's up bro?" Jade asked Flo.

"What's up sis?"

"Shit'd, just chilling," she said excusing herself to take a shower.

"Look bruh," Flo flexed showing me his brand new Audemars Piguet.

"Damn bruh, that bitch nice, how much that bitch cost you?"

"A lil bit of nothing, I got you one to mane…" Flo stated showing me the matching watch. "You know we gotta show out tonight, it's Rick Rick birthday. We're going to take over Club O,

Omar know the owner, 'Fat Sosa,' he gone let us in with the blicks. I already pre-ordered about 50 bottles! It's Friday we in it," Flo stated excitedly.

"I'm with it," I replied.

"I got some mo good news to though bruh, you remember Big Greg that own the bar we looked at?"

"Yea bruh, that muthafucka was big," I replied.

"Well, he's ready to sell that bitch and said he'll take hundred-thousand cash."

"That sound good, but we still got to get it appraised, plus he gone want some clean money," I replied.

"Yeah, I know and I got the perfect person for the job," he smiled.

"Who?" I asked.

"Queena," he stated.

"Queena?" I asked confused, "our cousin?"

"Yeah, nigga, Queena our cousin," he replied. "That's her line of work, that's what she went to school for, and she been dying to get to the States."

"I didn't know that, but sounds good. See what you can make happen, we can really turn that bitch up," I stated.

"I was thinking about turning that bitch into a strip club with an eatery inside, we can get some of the best bitches around the world to dance in that bitch for us. We can name that bitch, Sasha's; and she can run that bitch when she gets out," Flo stated confidently.

"I like the sound of that, imma hit you when I get in traffic."

"Bet bruh," Flo replied and then hung up.

The block was busy and traffic was everywhere, you would think it was a block party but nawl, it was just how good the product was. Lil Prince sat on the hood of his Candy Red s550 Benz. Kids was riding up and down the block on their new bikes that was complimentary to the Mud-brothers. They also bought the older kids motor scooters. Lil Prince name was starting to ring harder than the rest of the gang because of his unfriendly nature and his quick trigger finger, and boyish features. Plus, the nigga stayed in the hood. Everyone knew Lil Zay was Lil Prince's protégé and the ten deaths in two hours was a direct retaliation behind Lil Zay's death.

Not to mention, he almost single handily took Baby and Mula block over, him and Rick Rick of course. He also became partners with Omar. Since Omar didn't have the money but he had his liquor license, Lil Prince paid to help expand the corner store. He paid to get the back remodel so that it can be expanded into a liquor store. He paid for the venders and he paid for all the liquor. Valo and Flo hooked up with Omar's lawyer name Desist Oceans, she specialized in money laundering. She also was the person to oversee all the Real estate purchases. She was the one responsible for closing the deal on the building that they were trapping out of.

They now owned that building and the two buildings next to them. Lil Prince actually did something that the rest of the gang knew nothing about. He had Omar upgraded the cameras outside of the store and strategically pointed them so that the whole block was being watch at all times without anyone besides him and Omar knowing. This was his leverage. Omar proved to be a real OG. He showed us young gangsters the business side of the game, he was like the God father to all of us. He showed us how to flip our money and how to network. We were slowly turning into a super group.

"Hey Valo..." a soft voice cooed. I looked up and it was Kiesha.

"What's up ma?" I replied. I liked Kiesha, she was a gangster.

"You Big Dog... I see you shinning," she said referring to my jewels.

I had to admit, the sun had my diamonds dancing. "Just a lil jewelry," I replied nonchalantly.

"I love me a humble ass nigga," she flirted. "You know Choppa got shot a few days ago," she stated.

"Choppa got shot?" I asked making a face.

"Yeah, somebody ran up in his spot, tied him up, then robbed and shot him. I'm so happy my sister wasn't there when that shit went down, there's no telling what would have happened," she said in a sad voice.

"And you saying this to say what?" I asked her.

"Because I thought you wanted to know everything that goes on around here."

"That shit happen around here?" I asked looking at her.

"Nawl, but it happens in the city and I heard that the DIME-BOYZ ran the city now," she stated in attempt to save face. I thought it was cute, I mean Kiesha was a bad bitch and she was a hustler, but I knew she was a thot. She was just on Flo's dick the other day, but that not going to stop me from wanting to smash her thick ass.

"So, what y'all on?" she asked me. "I heard y'all was taking over Club O tonight."

"Yeah, it's Rick Rick's birthday and we going to do it big for the homie," I boasted.

"Well, we will definitely be in that bitch," she stated all ghetto like. "No wonder y'all niggas tore up the Gucci store like that," she stated referring to the 50k we spent in the designer store. "That's all the hoes in the salons were talking about today, y'all got hoes thirsty."

"Yeah, ma, you know we do our thang," I stated. Just then a thick ass brown skin chick walked up.

"Hey girl," she stated.

"Hey girl," Kiesha replied. "Valo this is Jockey, Jockey this is Valo."

"Hi," she said reaching her manicured hand out. I shook her hand. *Oh, my God, this bitch was bad,* I thought. She was about 5'6, thick light brown skin with a pretty face and a big ole ass. I definitely liked what I saw.

"This here is my girl, she coming to help celebrate at the club tonight."

"Good," I said with lust in my eyes. I could feel her sizing me up too. "Where you from ma? I never seen you around here."

"I'm from Atlanta, I'm just down here visiting."

"ATL huh, shawty?" I asked her trying to sound like TI. She smiled at my attempt of humor. "Look, let me know when y'all get there so y'all don't have to stand in that long ass line, call my phone and imma make sure y'all V.I.P like us."

"Nigga, we are V.I.P," Kiesha joked, "but I will." She stated winking at me. For some reason I had a good feeling about tonight

# Chapter (11)

The club was packed, the turnout was unbelievable. It seemed like the whole city came out for the event. Niggas from the South, West, North and Eastside was all in attendance. Niggas from Tampa Bay, Orlando, Miami Beach, even South Beach came to show love. Florida was definitely the place to be. All the major players were out. The parking lot was full of foreign cars and bad bitches, you could smell the weed smoke in the air. The women were dressed in next to nothing. Biggs pulled into the parking lot with two bad bitches draped on his arm. He was dressed in designer gear from head to toe. He was definitely in his bag now thanks to Stevo and the **DIME-BOYZ**.

He wasn't going to miss this party for nothing in the world. The barber shops, the salons and most of all social media platforms such as Facebook, Twitter, Instagram, and Snap Chat was buzzing about the hood affair. This was officially the first time that the **DIME-BOYZ** was showing their faces to the public. A lot of people have heard rumors about the group, but very few people knew how they looked. Biggs was iced out, he had on at least fifth-thousand in jewelry, the diamonds on his neck and wrist was sparkling. He pimped walked out of the parking lot and pass the long line of eager party goers, the line was wrapped around the corner. Making it to the front of the line Biggs walked up to the bouncer. The bouncer was about just as big as he was.

"Name?" the bouncer asked in a menacing voice.

"Biggs..." Biggs stated confidently.

"Biggs?" the bouncer asked checking his list. "Funny, I don't see no Biggs on this muthafucka."

"What?" Biggs barked stepping closer to the bouncer, "You better check that muthafucka again nigga," Biggs stated confidently. Not the one to back down, the bouncer stepped a little closer to Biggs.

"I said there isn't no Biggs on this muthafucka, so get yo big ass to the back of the line like everybody else chump." Biggs balled his fist up but was stopped by one of the women that was with him.

"Baby it's okay, we can just get in line," the woman stated unsure knowing how Biggs's temper can be. She knew it was a possibility that if they went to the back of the line that it would take hours to get into the club.

"You know what? Your right baby, we can get in the back of the line."

Biggs pretended as if he was about to walk away, but with lighting speed turned around with a powerful right hook hitting the bouncer and actually knocking him off his feet, and knocking him out cold.

"Nigga you know who the fuck I am?" Biggs barked at the unconscious man as he began to kick him in the face. About three bouncers rushed out of the club headed Biggs's way.

Just as they were about two feet away, Biggs went into his waist line and pulled out a baby Draco; and as if on que the two women he was with came outta they purse with baby nines.

"Buck muthafucka," the shorter dark skin woman name Stacy stated aiming her gun ready for whatever.

This cause the crowd to step back a little. The bouncers stood frozen with fear, the club door aggressively opened and non-other than the man himself 'Fat Sosa' emerged. He was a chubby Italian mob boss that left the crime life alone and came to Miami to go legit, but opportunities kept presenting themselves. He was still very much as dangerous as they come.

"Biggs," Fat Sosa asked in his accent, "what seems to be the problem?"

"This muthafucka disrespected me, said I wasn't on the list and called me a chump," Biggs stated out of breath.

Fat Sosa looked at the delirious simi-conscious bouncer on the floor. "Mike," he said referring to one of the bouncers, "take him to the back," he ordered. "Biggs, can you please lower your weapon? You're scarring my customers." Fat Sosa asked politely looking at Biggs and his girls.

"My bad man," Biggs said looking at the ladies and causing them to also lower their weapons.

"Oh, my God look?" a woman yelled.

Gliding down the block was two all-white on white stretch Range Rovers. The trucks were heavily tinted and luxurious. Both trucks pulled up directly in front of the club and all the commotion.

The first person to step out of the truck was Stevo and the birthday boy himself, Rick Rick. The whole gang decided to wear all white Gucci lenient.

One by one the DIME-BOYZ emerged from the trucks clean as a whistle. Dee Dee was the biggest surprise of them all. Tokyo talked her into getting dressed up. She pampered her and gave her a dramatic makeover.

"Girl, you so pretty let me make you over."

"I don't know Toke," Dee Dee replied. An hour after constant pressure Dee Dee finally gave in, she was a little tomboyish, but in a dress like she had on you would never knew unless you knew her.

She wore a Gucci dress that showed off her curves. Even the gang had a hard time taking their eyes off her. They never seen her dress so sexy. She really outdid herself, she had her hair washed, conditioned, and pressed, once finished her hair was at least 22 inches, her eye lashes and eye brows were done fresh, her hair came down to the middle of her back. She had on red bottom heels, a custom Gucci dress with the matching Gucci purse to go with it. There was no secret what she had inside it. *"Safety first…"* she always thought. She also wore a tennis bracelet and a custom tennis chain that read 'DIME-GIRL.' She was truly beautiful.

The whole gang was iced out with DIME-BOYZ chains and bitches started taking pictures like they were celebrities.

"Biggs my nigga," Stevo spoke walking up shaking his hand with his dreads hanging down the middle of his back. "What's good my nigga you straight?"

"Yeah, I'm cool mane, just had to knock this muthafucken bouncer out, nothing major," he replied shaking Stevo's hand.

Now the whole gang was standing at the door Valo, Flo, Ondat, Dee Dee, Rick Rick, Lil Prince, and Stevo.

"Welcome, welcome, welcome, come right in, sorry for the inconvenience," Fat Sosa spoke trying to break the tension. One of the bouncers opened up the door to the club making room for the gang.

With the amount of money, they spent on the event, Fat Sosa made a mental note to go out his way to make sure they were comfortable. With Biggs and his two bitches in tow, the super group proceed to mob into the establishment, as promised no one was searched. Walking into the club was like entering into another world, it was plush! On the first floor, there were three fully stocked bars circling around the dance floor, with another room connected to the stage that was actually, another bar with a TV inside the room. The whole room had mirror tint on the outside, but on the inside was a window that showed the whole stage; so, people thought that they were dancing in front of a mirror. In actuality, they were dancing in front of a room full of people, it was pretty cool.

The club was two stories, the second floor over looked the whole club, and the best part was that the floor on the second floor was some type of glass which made it see through, so if you were on the first floor you could look up and see all the action, especially the women that wore dresses. You could actually tell what color panties they were wearing, if they were wearing any. It was also equipped with two bars with all of the top shelf bottles of liquor and champagne. It was mostly reserved for very important people, and this is where the **DIME-BOYZ** section was located.

The music was blaring, the bass was thumping and the dance floor was shaking. One of the latest songs from Lil Durk was playing and the club was going up. The second floor was made lavishly, the section that the **DIME-BOYZ** was in was like a mini club itself. It had plush leather sofas, see through tables, about fifty bottles of everything scattered around for everybody to drink. All the big dogs that the **DIME-BOYZ** was serving cocaine to was already there.

Once Valo and the gang made it to the V.I.P section, everybody went wild showing mad love. There was a bunch of familiar faces in attendance, it was a lotta love being shown, a lotta hands being shook. Bitches was waiting outside the rope in hopes of being around the real ballers. It was also a lot of people that they didn't recognized in attendance iced out, the wheels in Lil Prince head was turning. One person that caught Lil Prince's eyes was Choppa, he was sitting with two dudes by his side that Lil Prince didn't recognized. They had three bottles at their table. He looked a little banged up, but he was walking.

*"Didn't Kiesha tell me this nigga just got shot..."* Lil Prince thought. Walking over to him Lil Prince decided to pick his brain.

"What's the word Choppa?" Prince asked.

"What's up Lil Prince mane, you look good baby."

"Can't say the same about you, what the fuck happened to you?"

"Man, some rookie muthafucka ran in my spot and caught me slipping, got a nigga good too. Popped me up and all type of shit, but I'm good now, the bulletproof vest I had on saved me, the rookie muthafucka didn't have heart to finish the job."

"Damn, that's fucked up, you know who did it?"

"Nah, not yet at least."

"You good?" Lil Prince asked sensing vulnerability in Choppa voice.

"Yeah, as far as that bullshit, I'm good, whoever did this gone wish they killed me. But I'm in a bad spot on the work side," Choppa stated.

"Don't worry about it, just hit me up and we can work something out," Prince stated.

One of the dudes that Choppa was with spit his drink up like he was choking or something.

"You okay nigga?" The other dude that was with Choppa asked.

"Yeah, I'm cool shit, must of went down the wrong pipe," Chase replied.

"Excuse me if I'm being rude, this my cousins Blac Vontay and his guy Chase, they're here from Atlanta."

*"Atlanta… what's up with all these muthafuckas from Atlanta today…"* Prince thought thinking of Jockey.

"Actually, I'm glad that you came over to show some love," Choppa stated truthfully.

He really didn't have no problem with Lil Prince, he didn't too much care for him, but he liked him more than the others. He liked how Lil Prince was about his business, he was young and ambitious. He kind of felt out of place because in all truth, he wasn't a part of the movement; he was just Tiffany's boyfriend.

"I was wondering when could we actually talk business. You know me, if it makes money it makes sense," Choppa joked.

Lil Prince looked at the two niggas that Choppa was with and told him, "I'll get with you," Lil Prince smiled.

Sensing the hesitation Choppa backed off. He was hoping to find some better prices and he felt like middle manning his cousin was the best way to get back on.

"Take down my number," Lil Prince stated, they exchanged numbers and Lil Prince walked off joining the gang.

"I don't know about that nigga," Chase spoke up, "that young nigga gives me the creeps."

"Yeah, man, he seems sneaky and the eyes don't lie," Black Vontay agreed.

"Nah man, Lil Prince cool, he about his paper, but he not to be fucked with so don't let them boyish features fool you, that young nigga mental," Choppa stated in a serious tone. "They say he was the one that kilt them ten people in two hours," Choppa added.

"Where you here that at?" Chase asked with fear evident in his voice.

"You know the streets talk."

"I remember seeing some shit like that on the news," Blac Vontay spoke up.

"Well, it doesn't matter because he gone be our Mil-Ticket, he gone plug us I with the work," Choppa stated.

*'Yup and imma rob his skinny ass, so this who yo plug is huh...'* Chase thought under his breath.

The party was a success, Dee Dee was having a hard time adjusting to the fact that she was beautiful. She felt bitter sweet about how muthafuckas was staring at her. She was ready to shoot a muthafucka, she turned down about twenty numbers because everybody wanted a piece of the first lady. They knew her status and how deadly she was, and for some reason that made them want her even more.

Dee Dee felt a body flopping down on the sofa next to her, she was ready to pop off until she realized it was Rick Rick.

"What's up sis, you look like you not having a good time, you straight?" he asked.

"Yeah, I'm good my boy, I'm having a ball, it's just these thirsty ass niggas that's getting on my fucking nerves. They acting like I'm Beyoncé in this bitch… they sweating a muthafucka, damn, can a bitch get some air?" she huffed.

"I'm not gone lie sis, you do look beautiful tonight," Rick Rick stated truthfully.

Hearing them words come from Rick Rick touched her soul because she knew he wasn't trying to get no pussy. She knew he meant every word. She just looked at him for a minute unsure what to say.

*'Maybe I am beautiful...'* she thought.

A Drake song came on that sent the club into a frenzy, Rick Rick grabbed Dee Dee's hand.

"Get yo ass up sis, you gone dance with me it's my B-Day."

"Boy, I don't fucking dance," Dee Dee laughed. Rick Rick gave her that it's my birthday look, again.

"Okay, what the fuck," Dee Dee smiled grabbing Rick Rick's hand causing a few niggas to groan in disapproval.

"Isn't this about a bitch? I've been asking that bitch to dance all night," some dude moaned under his breath.

Seeing Rick Rick trying to dance had the whole gang laughing. All the niggas that was trying to get Dee Dee's attention was jealous. But it loosens Dee Dee up and before you knew it the party turnt up, everyone had a blast. Tiffany, Jade, Jockey, and Kiesha showed up and showed out. All of them was on the dance floor shaking ass and turning up with the gang. They let a few bitches that was on the other side of the rope in and thangs got a little wilder from there.

Ondat was in a private room getting sucked and fucked with a white and a black bitch. Stevo, Tokyo, and Yoku was smoking some of the best weed while recording everything. Valo was getting Jade drunk as fuck, they were kissing, licking, and touching each other on the sofa; it was safe to say that they needed a room. Kiesha and Jockey was acting like they wanted to have a threesome with Lil Prince, they were both sitting on his lap. Flo was making money moves. He found four new buyers and some hungry lil shooters from Milwaukee that he took a liking to, which was rare.

He as a gang only type nigga, but for some reason these lil nigga captivated him. He invited them to V.I.P. and was impress that they had enough clout to even get in the club only being seventeen and eighteen years old. Leaving the club, Flo, Stevo, Rick Rick, Dee Dee, and Ondat packed one of the Rovers with bitches. The gang had the driver bring all of them to the Airbnb. Valo went with Jade, Lil Prince went with Jockey and Kiesha as they all piled into Jockey's car. Unbeknownst to him, they were being followed.

## Chapter (12)

*'I got this nigga…'* Chase thought as he followed the car Lil Prince was in from a safe distance. He was in a stolen S.U.V with dark tints, thanks to Tiffany. She didn't know what he was up to, but she didn't ask to many questions and just provided him with the car. She enjoyed having a partner in crime. She didn't want Choppa to get wind of the conversations her and Chase was having, nor did she want Choppa to know that she was the one who set him up for Chase to rob and shoot him. She was honestly happy that Chase didn't kill Choppa. She was kinda feeling him a little now especially, since he survived that hit.

Chase ditched Choppa, Tiffany, and Blac Vontay pretending that he was leaving with a woman he met in the club, in all actuality he was following Lil Prince. Chase once asked Tiffany could she set one of the DIME-BOYZ up?

"What? Nigga is you fucking stupid, that's a death wish," she screamed. "Them niggas is off limits!"

"Come on shawty, just one of them niggas?"

"What part you don't understand, the N or the O," Tiffany huffed angrily.

*'We'll see…'* Chase deviously thought. "Them DIME-BOYZ niggas bleed like we do shawty," Chase replied.

"I knew you was fucking crazy, nigga they are off limits end of discussion," she stated on her way out of Chase's hotel room.

Jockey navigated through traffic sloppily, she was feeling herself because she honestly had one, too many drinks. Lil Prince demanded the keys from Jockey,

"I'll drive ma," he stated.

She handed him the keys without thinking twice. He made a right pulling down a long block and parked. He was unaware of the danger that was lurking behind the stolen car that was following them. He was usually on point, but celebrating with the gang had him very tipsy.

*'Yeah, pull over shawty…'* Chase thought. Pulling down his mask Chase checked his twin bitches. He brought the stolen car to

a slow creep. Looking for a place to park, he saw Lil Prince getting out of the car with the two bitches.

*'Damn, he getting away...'* Chase thought, "fuck it," he said to himself throwing the car in park in the middle of the street. "Off limits my ass," he smirked. Chase hopped out of the car catching Lil Prince totally by surprise

"Put yo muthafucken hands where I can see them nigga!" Chase demanded. Lil Prince threw his hands up in the air. "You bitches too," he barked pointing his gun at both Kiesha and Jockey. Lil Prince was strapped but Chase had the ups on him. Chase walked up to Lil Prince and disarmed him.

"Look my man, you don't know who I am so I'm gone give you a chance to leave with yo life, just walk away," Lil Prince slurred. Chase looked at Lil Prince from behind his mask.

"What nigga? You think this shit a joke?" He asked striking Lil Prince in the face with the butt of the gun and drawing blood above his left eye. "Nigga give me this chain," he barked taking Lil Prince's chain off his neck. "Give me this phone too," he continued as he robbed him. He also took all the money outta Lil Prince's pocket, the whole ordeal only took 2-3 minutes.

"Where the real money at? Take me in the crib I want everything nigga."

Out of the blue a light came on from a house across the street as he was talking causing Chase to panicked. Chase looked Lil Prince in the eyes, "I'll see you again," Chase Smiled.

For some strange reason he didn't search the women which would prove to be a costly mistake. When he turns around Kiesha upped her pink 380 and began blasting.

"Oh, shit..." Chase yelled barley dodging a bullet to the head.

"You bitch ass nigga!" Kiesha yell busting her gun. Running for cover Chase began shooting back causing Lil Prince and Jockey to take cover.

Chase made it to his car and before he was able to shut the door he was rammed from behind.

"You leaving so soon?" the teenagers asked with a smile on their face.

Flo hit it off with the young goons right away. Flo easily could spot a killer from anywhere. The duo definitely stuck out like sore thumbs at the party. He decided to pick their brain. He immediately saw the empty look in their eyes and he reflected on the day that the Feds took Sasha away. He remembered that same look when he looked in the mirror for a long while after that. He knew two things for sure, he was either gone have to put them on his team or kill them one day. Once he began talking to them he realized how much they reminded him of him and Valo.

They were from Milwaukee, and on the run for a homicide. They were both looking to put in work and getting paid, they were truly lost. Flo didn't drink much at the club because he had to stay on point, he noticed Lil Prince getting a little tipsy and asked the boys to watch over him as their first job. Akil, better known as Kill was seventeen and the deadliest one. Shootsum was eighteen and just as deadly, they were cousins. They already knew who Valo, Flo, and the DIME-BOYZ was by name and they really believed in their movement. They'd heard about the ten murders in two hours and idolized the gang for it.

They were eager to prove themselves and be down with the winning team. Flo picked them up on the spot and their first assignment was to make sure Lil Prince got home safe. They actually pulled up just in time. Ramming Chase's stolen S.U.V with a stolen F250 of their own.

"Ah, shit…" Chase yelled as his head slammed into the steering wheel from the impact. He recovered quickly though and threw the car in drive and sped off with the youngans on his hills. Shootsum was driving, he considered himself a tipper or a graze, terms they use in Milwaukee if you were a good driver. He was used to getting in high speed chases with the Milwaukee Police Department.

Turning the corner Chase side swiped a parked car. **Foc, Foc, Foc,** his back window shattered, Kill was aiming to kill. Chased ducked down and floored the gas peaking over the dashboard just enough for him to see where he was going. He ran a stop sign and boom, he was hit hard by a civilian who had the right away causing his car to spend outta control and crash into another parked car. He felt blood leaking from his head and tremendous pain in his left shoulder, but he thugged it out. He hopped out on foot and began running through the gang ways. He dropped everything he took from Lil Prince except the gun, he knew better then to drop that, he already had two guns on him. He didn't even look back he was just hauling ass. **Boom, boom, boom** he heard the shots whizzing pass his head, he fired shots behind him without even looking back. He heard the youngans chasing him, he had a nice lead on them and he jumped a fence ended up in a nice backyard with a patio door.

He didn't feel he had the energy to hop the other fence so he checked the patio door, and to his luck the door was open. He eased his way inside and locked the door then peeked out of the window. He could hear the youngans talking.

"Damn dog, which way did he go?"

"I don't know dog, I think he jumped the fence."

"He didn't run in this house, did he?"

"I don't think so, check and see if the patio door open."

Chase had his gun at the ready, he prepared his self for a shootout.

"Naw, its locked."

"Fuck dog, let's get out here, we got the chain and shit back. Fuck it, let's go and return this shit."

'Damn...' Chase thought to himself, all of this shit for nothing.

Turning around, he was met by an older black woman with a 44. bull dog pointed to his face.

"Who the fuck is you, and what the fuck are you doing in my house?"

Chase put his hands up.

"Drop the gun." she stated. She looked to be around 49-50 years old, she had long salt and pepper hair that was pulled into a pony tail, she had wide hips and a big booty, alongside with some nice size breast. You could tell that she was a bad bitch in her days because she was still nice to look at and could easily pass for 35-40.

He put the gun down. "Now, kick it over to me." He kicked her the gun. "Start talking nigga."

"I'm soooooo sorry mama, some dudes were after me and I just ran. I'm from outta town so I didn't have no were to run to, I don't even know where I'm at. They tried to car jack me and I just ran," he said without taking a breath.

"Got some ID?" she asked turning on the light never taking the gun off him. He reached in his pocket and threw her his wallet.

"Atlanta huh?" she asked letting her guard down a little. "Your bleeding," she stated.

"I know, I hit my head on the steering wheel," Chase replied.

"No, not your head your chest."

It seemed like as soon as she mentioned that he was bleeding Chase felt a burning sensation in his chest, and then his shoulder, so he lifted his shirt up and he hadn't known he was shot until now. All of the sudden, everything became dizzy and he passed out

Twelve hours later Chase awoke with a confused state of mind. It was about 3.00pm and he was unaware of where he was. He looks at his surrounding and the room was unfamiliar. He had on a thick fluffy robe and he was lying in a comfortable queen side bed. He notices he was naked under his robe. He tried moving and felt a sharp pain in his shoulder. He also had a small bandage above his eye.

*Last night...*' he thought, then everything started coming back to him, the robbery, the chase, the lady. Just then, in walked Dr. Griffen. She also had on a thick white robe.

"Look who's up," she smiled. Chase jumped. "Your safe baby, the bullet went in and out, and I patched you up really good."

"Thanks," Chase replied. Ms. Griffen brought him a glass of orange juice and some pain killers, along with a cell phone.

"You know you're in Miami, you can't be just running into anybody's house like you did last night, I could have killed you."

"I know," Chase replied.

"Your safe now, and your three guns are in the bag," she said pointing at the bag sitting in the chair. "How do you feel?" she asked him.

"I could be better, but could be worse," Chase smiled.

"Okay, imma give you some privacy to make a call, here's the address to where you are," she said handing him a piece of paper.

She walked off and Chase couldn't help but stare at her ass that was peeking out from under her robe. She was forty-eight with a few love handles but over all in good shape. Her ass was soooooo fat. He was in a trance watching her walk away.

*'She can't have on no panties,'* Chase thought and felt his dick getting hard. He tried taking his mind off her, but he couldn't and his morning boner wouldn't go down.

He made a call to Blac Vontay and arranged for him to come get him. Dr. Griffen walked back in with a pair of sweats,

"Here you go, these are some of my son clothes he wears them when he comes in town, but I'm pretty sure he wouldn't mind," she blushed. She began looking around the room nervously.

"Thank you."

"Ummm, my name is Ruby, but everyone calls me Doc, that's what the folks at the nail shop calls me anyway," she blushed again.

"Thanks, Ms. Ruby, I can never repay you, you saved my life."

He stood up and finally notice why she was acting so strange. His dick was sticking out from under his robe, he was about nine inches long and thick. He covered up,

"I'm sooo sorry mama, I didn't notice it was out," Chase stated embarrassed.

"It's okay," she smiled. "However, there is a way you can repay an old woman like me." She stepped closer batting her eyes.

Feeling the vibe his dick jumped. He didn't even know he was attracted to older women, but he knew for sure that if she threw it he was catching it. She opens her robe revealing that she didn't have on anything under it.

*'Nice...'* Chase thought.

She walked up to him and opened his robe. He just stood there like a God while she rubbed and kissed his chest, and his hard six pack. He had a body of a God and he took pride in keeping his self-up. She was about 5'6 so Chase tall frame towered over her. She began kissing his neck and he grabbed her big soft booty cheeks, she moaned loving the feeling of his big hands firmly gripping her fluffy cheeks. She started sucking on his nipples and a soft moan escaped his mouth. He'd never had his nipples sucked and the strange feeling actually felt good to him. She grabbed his dick and began jagging it slowly while sucking his nipples.

He grabbed her head and they began kissing. He turned her around and bent her over the bed. She laid her face flat on the bed sideways with her ass in the air. He opened her big soft booty cheeks and eased his dick inside her.

"Oh, shit…" she moaned, "baby take it easy on mama it's been a while." Unbeknownst to him she, haven't had sex in the last two years and the dick wasn't half of his size. He was surprise at how tight her pussy was.

"Damn shawty, this pussy tight as fuck," Chase moaned slow stroking her pussy.

"Oh, shit baby fuck me…" Ms. Ruby moaned. He began long dicking her. "Oh, shit that's it, put that whole dick in mama," she moaned. Chase began speeding up.

"I'm cumming babyyyyy…" she moaned creaming on his dick.

*Damn, this some good pussy…*' Chase thought fucking her harder.

"Yes, that's it baby, fuck me I can take it," she moan.

"Ah shit ma, you gone take this dick like a big girl," he moaned smacking her on the ass. She came on his dick again.

"Yes, oh, God yes, imma take it like a big girl spank me." He grabbed her hips and began fucking her with lighting speed and spanking her. He slowly stuck a finger in her ass as he was fucking her.

"Oh, shit yes, don't stop fuck me daddy, oh, my God that's my spot," she moaned.

"Shit ma, I'm about to cum…" he moaned as he pulled her hair.

"Keep that finger in my ass baby," she demands. Chase fingered her ass and she began squirting. The feeling was too much for Chase, he pulled out and began cumming all over her ass.

"Oh, my God," he moaned still stroking his dick. He was spent, but his dick was still hard. She showed him where the shower was at and he showered but not before he bent her over in the shower and went for round two.

"How long you in town?" she asked him handing him his bag of guns after they'd showered.

"I'm gone be here," he smiled.

"Here," she handed him a business card. It read 'Dr. Ruby Griffin,' "call me any time," she smiled.

"Most definitely," he flirted.

Chase opened the bag and put his twin bitches on his waist. He reached back in the bag and grabbed the gun he took from Lil Prince and checked the clip, it was full. It was a golden gun, *'Damn, this bitch looks familiar...'* he thought.

"Nah, this can't be?" He cocked it back to examine the barrel and it read Jimbo. *'I'll be damn...'* he thought.

"How the fuck did Lil Prince get Jimbo's gun?" He whispered to himself. *'I know for a fact this Jimbo's gun because me and Blac Vontay gave him this muthafucka for his birthday. Okay, now we getting somewhere...'* he thought. Shit just got real.

*'Damn, I can't believe I left my phone in a stolen car...'* he thought. As if on que, Dr. Ruby Griffin phone rung. She handed it to Chase.

"I'm outside mane."

"Okay, but mane I got some shit to tell you."

"Yeah?" Blac Vontay asked.

"Yeah, mane, I think I might have found Jimbo's killer," Chase smiled.

## Chapter (13)
## - Flo -

It was about 9:00am, the sky was dark gray from the rain that was pouring down. The lightening was flashing and the thunder was roaring violently. Flo was sitting in bed at his condominium smoking a big blunt of exotic weed. He had a lot on his mind. He couldn't figure out who had the balls to rob Lil Prince. Everybody knew how the DIME-BOYZ was coming, they knew we had the streets on smash. The crazy thing is, if I wouldn't have put my lil homies on the job of making sure Lil Prince got home safe, there's no telling what would have happened. That's what bothers me more. They got all of Lil Prince's shit back, but most important, they got the nigga who did it cell phone.

Lil homie'nem must've really been on his ass for him to drop all that shit outside of the car. Only thing about it was that, Omar couldn't get into it because it was an iPhone, but we had a couple of leads though, so far, we knew it was an out of towner, a muthafucka from Atlanta. The nigga phone kept ringing and all the numbers coming in was from an Atlanta area code. So far, the number that was calling the most was a broad name Eraneka Sims, according to the phone records. Omar had the bitch looked up and about ten of them popped up in that same area, but by her age and the way she sounded on her voice mail, we were able to narrow it down to just three.

Stevo was already on it, him and Rick Rick flew out to Atlanta this morning. That's what made me order my lil hittas to snatch that lil bitch Jockey up. I mean she just popped up around the gang and one of the guys get robbed. Two plus two equal four, plus that bitch is from Atlanta, no ducks around here, something not right. I got the call about twenty minutes ago from Shootsum, telling me to meet him at the bando. That could only mean one thing, they got the bitch! I called Lil Prince to come pick me up, he was with Kiesha when he arrived. For twenty minutes I sat back in the plush leather seats of Kiesha's BMW and looked out the window.

Riding through the streets of Miami was no different from riding through Tampa Bay, Lil Haiti, Chicago, New York. Ghettos all around the world was the same. We made it to the bando (abandoned house) in record time. We walked into the room that she was tied up in. She had on a blind fold and she was stripped down in just her panties and bra tied to a chair. There was a gigantic fish tank full of water and a pair of curling irons plugged up next to it. I walked up to her and took her blind fold off, she looked at me with horror in her eyes.

"Valo, what's this about?" She asked mistaken me for my brother.

"You know what's this about bitch," Lil Prince replied smacking the shit outta her. I squatted down so that we were eye level.

"Now, I'm going to ask you one time, who sent you?"

"Who sent me? I don't understand, what do you mean?" Jockey cried. Keisha walked up and punched her in the face.

"Bitch, don't play dumb, who the fuck sent you? I haven't seen you all this time and you just pop up and my people get robbed? Bitch, I'm gone asks you this one mo time, who sent you?"

"I don't know what y'all talking about," she cried.

Kill laughed hard causing everybody to look at him.

"What's so funny?" Kiesha asked him not amused at all.

"This bitch lying," he said walking up to her and grabbed her by the neck, "I don't got all day bitch, and you wanna play these games huh?"

"No, I swear on my son I don't know what you guys are talking about."

"Suit yourself," Kill replied letting her neck go and walking over to the curling irons. He turned them on high and everybody was just starring at him.

*'What he gone do, electrocute the bitch...'* Lil Prince thought. Honestly, Lil Prince didn't think she had anything to do with it.

Kill walked back up to Jockey, her legs were tied to both legs of the chair so her legs were wide open. He stood in front of her with the curling irons.

"I'm gone ask you one mo time bitch, because I got shit to do, who the fuck sent you to rob my people?"

"I swear I haven't done anything wrong!"

"Okay, bitch, I told you," Kill stated.

He pulled her panties to the side and expose her shaved cat. She tried to wiggle away but she was tied down to tight. He then stuck the curling irons in her pussy, although they weren't hot yet, every second that passed they were getting hotter.

"Now, I don't know if you know how curling irons work but, every second you play dumb with me the hotter them muthafuckas gone get, eventually burning your shit inside out. Now, get to talking bitch, but before you lie let me show you something." He then placed a plastic bag over her head and tied it up. She felt the curling irons getting hotter and she was also struggling to breath, shit was getting real.

Flo was enjoying his lil mans at work, he was standing there like a proud father, *'good call...'* he thought to himself.

Kill picked her phone up outta her purse and used her finger print to open it up. He strolled down to a text that caught his eyes earlier. Meanwhile, Jockey was struggling to breath into the bag, she was pulling the bag into her face every time she breathed in, she was suffocating. Kill walked back over to Jockey and snatched the bag off her head. She began gasping for air. The air was starting to smell like burnt flesh, the curling irons was heating up.

"Okay," kill yelled strolling down Jockey text messages. Message from C: (where are you?) Jockey: (I'm with him now) C: (Did you spike his drink yet?) Jockey: (I can't, he too much on point) C: (well, think of something, suck that nigga dick or sum) Jockey: (he invited me and Kiesha back to his place, just follow us he kinda tipsy too!)

"You bitch!" Lil Prince yelled, walking over to punch her in the mouth and knocking out one of her teeth. The smell of burned flesh was becoming overwhelming.

"Okay, okay, I'll talk, I'll talk," Jockey cried. "Please take the curling irons out of me they melting my pussy," Jockey cried hysterically.

"About time stupid ass bitch," Shootsum blurted, "I know your pussy on fire," he laughed.

"Talk bitch," Lil Prince yelled vexed.

"It was C, he put me up to it," she stated in obvious pain. "He flew me out from Atlanta and it was a coincident that I knew

Kiesha, we went to high school together. So, he suggests that was my way in to get to y'all through her, he wanted me to help him get close to anyone of you guys to rob. He said he'd been fucked up and needed some money because he was down bad. I'm so sorry…"

"Who the fuck is C?" I barked.

"Valo please take this outta me," she begged Flo still thinking he was Valo.

"Bitch, who the fuck is C and were that nigga at?" I barked.

She began going in and out of consciousness. I took the curling irons out of her pussy which was now leaking blood, you could see the brunt flesh on them. Kiesha threw a bucket of water on Jockey.

"Stay woke bitch," Kiesha spat.

"C and I was lovers in Atlanta," she whispered. "I knew he came to Miami so I hit him up."

"Who number is this that keep calling?" I asked showing her his phone. Eyes barely open she looked at it.

"That number look familiar, I think that's Blac baby momma number, actually, I'm sure it is."

"Eraneka Sims?" I asked.

"Yes, that's Nene," she replied.

"Who the fuck is Blac?" Lil Prince asked. "Blac is C's best friend, he could be calling him from his baby momma phone, they both came down here together," Jockey stated.

"Blac and his baby momma?" I asked. "No, Blac and C," she whispered.

"Okay, do you have Blac number?"

"No, I don't, but they supposed to be staying with his cousin."

"What's his cousin name?" I asked her.

She looked at Kiesha. Kiesha looked back at her,
"Talk bitch."

"Choppa," she blurted. The room went silent.

"Choppa?" Lil Prince asked.

"Tiffany's Choppa, the nigga that was at the party?"

"How Choppa look?" Kiesha asked. "Was he at the party?"

"He's a big nigga," she stated.

"Was he at the party?" Lil Prince spoke up.

"Yeah, he was," she replied in a low tone.

"Blac and C was too..." she continued.

"Muthafucka," Lil Prince yelled getting amped up. "I saw them niggas gang, I met them niggas bruh, Choppa introduced me to them niggas, I had a conversation with that nigga and we exchanged numbers and everything. I'm gone kill this nigga," Lil Prince snapped.

They were unaware that Choppa didn't have anything to do with it or any knowledge about the incident, they were just out for blood.

"Anything else you need to tell us?" Kiesha asked pointing the gun in Jockey face.

"C told me that he was working with a girl and she was pulling all the strings, she's from right here in Miami, I don't know her name though."

"Anything else?" Kiesha asked her, she was surprisingly clam.

"I'm so sorry, I never meant for this to happen..."

"Blah, blah, blah..." Kiesha mocked and raised the gun and repeatedly shot Jockey in the face until the clip was empty. "Bitch, don't you ever fuck with the gang," she stated kicking Jockey's dead body.

The way she handled herself, you would have never guessed that this was her first body. We all stood there with our mouths opened.

"Lil homie," I stated referring to Kill and Shootsum, "take care of this mess and call me when you're done. I got another mission for you." I handed him the Gucci bag containing the thirty-thousands I had for them.

"Thanks dog," they both replied.

"Yo, we out..." I stated to the gang and we mobbed out that bitch with murder on our minds.

* * *

# - Blac Vontay -

**I** couldn't believe what I was hearing. I was sitting in my hotel room with Chase and he was running down the events that took place last night.

"So, the nigga got salty over a bitch?" I asked confused.

"Yeah, mane, dat nigga was on some straight sucka shit mane. I mean, I didn't even know that the nigga was following me until I was at the bitch house," Chase lied. "I jumped out the car and three niggas ran up on me, including that nigga Lil Prince, and tried to get me. They didn't know I had my twin bitches with me though. I up my shit and them bitch ass niggas tried to run, I got to busting at they ass, we exchanged gun fire but that's when we heard police siren and we all went our separate ways. The bitch tried to run the nigga Lil Prince over and that's when he dropped this..." he said showing the golden gun.

"She stopped the car, so I get out and grab it thinking it's just a regular gun. I wake up this morning and examined it and that's when I notice it was Jimbo's shit," Chase lied. "Then, when the niggas were shooting at me they were like, 'we gone do you like we did that nigga Choppa.'"

"What?" I stated hopping up, "So, them the bitch ass niggas that robbed and shot my cousin?"

"Them dime limit niggas robbed and killed our mans too. How you think them niggas got on?" Chase continued. "Remember, Choppa said them niggas was some broke ass niggas and they just came up out the blue."

Yeah, I remember," I agreed.

"Shit making sense to you now mane?" Chase asked me.

"Yeah, mane, them niggas violated in a major way, we need to come up with a way to bake a cake for they ass," I answered. "I got an idea bruh," I replied.

I called Choppa and he picked up on the third ring.

"Yo," he answered.

"Mane, we need to meet up asap," I told him.

"I'm at the trap come through," he replied.

We pulled up to his house like an hour later. He was there by his self. We ran the story down to him and he was in disbelief.

"So, them the slimy muthafuckas that shot and robbed me? They must don't know who the fuck I am and why I adopted the moniker Choppa! I knew them lil bitch ass niggas was hating on me. Imma show these muthafuckas something," Choppa stated pulling out his phone. "They got life fucked up, I'm from Fort Myers."

Choppa made a call to his Choppa city niggas.

"Yo, who this?" a deep southern voice boomed.

"This Choppa."

"Choppa, what's up mane, how you holding up? I heard about that shit them fuck niggas pulled down there, I'm still disappointed in that shit, you straight?" the unknown voice asked.

"Not really, that's why I was kinda calling."

"I'm listening," the unknown voice replied.

"I found out who did that shit."

"Awe yeah?"

"Yeah."

"Okay, what do you need, you know we Choppa city baby."

"I need you to send me some muscle, these niggas kinda got the streets on lock."

"Yeah, sound profitable."

"It is," Choppa replied with a smile on his face. "I was thinking, once we smash these lil niggas we can take over they spots."

"Yeah, that shit sound good, imma send Hitman'nem."

"Perfect, thanks big homie I owe you one."

"Don't sweat it we're family, but watch over my people Hitman especially, he hasn't been the same since that shit happen."

"I will big homie I got you."

"Okay, sounds good."

"Okay, imma send my location."

"I already know where it's at."

'Damn...' Choppa thought. "Okay, sounds good, imma call you when they touch down."

"Say no mo, one..."

"What was that about?" I asked.

Choppa smiled, "Them niggas wanna go to war imma show them how Choppa city niggas do it."

"I was thinking, don't yo bitch run with them niggas?" Chase asked.

"I mean, she doesn't run with them, but they stay in the same building. She cool with them niggas though."

"You thinking what I'm thinking?" Chase asked Choppa with a smirk on his face.

Choppa smiled, "as a matter of fact I am, it's about time this bitch chooses her side."

"I like the sound of that, get her on the phone," Chase added.

"Now, are you sure it was them niggas that tried to rob you?" I asked.

"What?" Chase jumped up. "You questioning my vision now Tay? Since, when have I jumped out of the window, I know what I heard and I know what I saw," he lied.

"I'm just saying, there is no turning back once we bit these niggas."

"Them niggas tried to rob and kill me, they robbed my man's Choppa, and they kilt Jimbo, enough is enough…" Chase bark.

"I'm with you mane," Choppa stood up shaking his hand.

"Let's do this, call Tiffany," Chase Stated.

"Bet," Choppa replied, "it's up there and its stuck there."

# Chapter (14)
## - Stevo -

**O**ur flight landed in Atlanta at approximately 4:25pm and I felt rejuvenated. Rick Rick was kinda sluggish, he claims he had jet leg but for the most part he was on point. We rented a brand-new infinity coup through one of Omar contacts. It was kinda flashy, but most important it was fast something we might needed. We both rocked our iced-out DIME-BOYZ chains and our Audemars Piguets. We both was dressed in designer gear, we most definitely looked like famous rappers. Most bitches say I looked like the late rapper 'OTF NuNu,' but I think it's just the dreads and the skin tone that make us similar.

We checked into the Ritz Carlton under fake names. We put our things away and went to meet Zahara, she was our gun connect through Biggs. The GPS notified us that we'd arrived. She lived in a nice small house right outside of Atlanta in a suburban area. I rung the door bell,

"Coming," a soft sweet voice yelled.

Zahara answered the door dressed comfortable, she was beautiful, to my surprise she was a white woman.

*"How Biggs know this fine ass white bitch..."* I thought.

She had blond hair, blue eyes, fake tits and all. She was gorgeous though and I must admit, I was intoxicated by her fragrance.

"You guys must be friends of Biggs?" she asked.

"I'm Rick Rick!" Rick stated.

"You must be Stevo?" She interrupted him holding her hand out to me, she shook our hands and invited us in. "How's Atlanta treating you guys so far?" she asked.

"So far so good," I replied.

"Can I offer you guys anything?" she asked.

"Nah, we straight ma, we just here for the blicks."

"Blicks," she smiled. "I never heard them put in that term before, must be a city thing?"

"Must be," Rick Rick replied dryly.

"Okay, follow me."

*"Damn, this white girl got ass..."* I thought as she walked in front of us.

I knew she knew we was watching her from behind because she put a little extra in her step. We followed her into the basement and she walked us into a room inside of a room. She then pushed a brick into the wall were a keypad was hidden, she punched in some numbers and the wall slid to the side exposing about 30 different guns, knives, and bullet proof vests.

"Take your picks," she smiled.

She walked off and we took our picks. I took a baby nine and a F&N, Rick Rick took two 40. Glocks with the switch on them. We were only here for a bitch, but bruh was on his better safe than sorry shit.

"Thanks, how much we owe you?" I flirted once she arrived back in the basement.

"Biggs took care of everything," she replied. "Here is my number if you guys need anything else while you're here, just call."

"I will do," I responded. She winked at me and we left.

We had some time to kill so we hit the mall. Walking through the mall of Atlanta was like walking through a fashion show. I mean there were bad bitches everywhere, everybody was fly. We walked in the Gucci store and there were three females and three dudes in there. From the way they were communicating, you could tell that they were all together.

All eyes were on us when we walked in. I shyly eased my hand next to my gun, these muthafuckas was looking at us like we were aliens or something. A small slim, cute black girl with braces walked up to us, she had to be about nineteen or twenty, and about 5'4.

"Hello, can I help you with anything?" She asked.

"Nah, we just looking right now," I replied, "but I'll let you know when we find something."

"Okay," she smiled walking off switching her little ass cheeks.

I looked at Rick Rick to see did he peep how they was looking at us, but he was already on point.

"I feel the vibe," he stated.

One of our onlookers looked to be about fifteen or sixteen years old, he was the one really watching us like a hawk.

"Say mane?" He finally spoke.

I just looked at him.

"That watch," he said pointing to my watch, "that muthafucka nice."

"Thanks Joe," I replied.

"Thanks Joe?" He questions, as in deep thought.

"Y'all from Chicago?" He asked.

"Yeah, we're just up here checking out y'all city," I replied. "Were the smoke at? Its dry as fuck out this bitch."

"We got the smoke, coke, whatever you need shawty. I'm Delyuntay," he put his hand out.

"Stevo," I replied shaking his hand.

"This my brother King Lando," he said referring to the dude walking up. I could feel him sizing me up.

"This Stevo." Delyuntay stated making the introduction. King Lando nodded his head.

"Nice watch," he stated.

"Thanks," I replied. I looked at his watch an noticed he had the exact same watch on and I smirked.

"They're from Chicago," Delyuntay spoke up. King Lando actually smiled.

"This my brother Rick Rick," I stated. They nodded at each other with Rick Rick still not speaking.

'Who the fuck is these niggas...' King Lando thought. '...*They only made ten of these watches, and both of them have one on, plus me, that mean its only seven more that exist, what am I missing? DIME-BOYZ...*' he thought looking at their chains. '...*I never heard of that, must be some Chicago shit...*'

"Y'all niggas got some smoke?" Rick Rick finally spoke up.

"As a matter of fact, we do. How long you niggas in town for shawty?"

"About two three days."

King Lando went into his Gucci bag and pulled out two zips of exotic weed and handed one to me and one to Rick. I pulled out a wad of money, but was immediately waved off.

"This on the house," King stated.

"Nah, it's cool," I replied trying to give him the money.

"Nah man, I insist," he replied. "Why don't y'all slide down to my club tonight if y'all not doing shit?"

He gave me his card and I took it.

"It may be beneficial," he winked.

*"What's up with all this winking shit…"* I thought.

We spent like 20k in the Gucci store altogether, we both bought a few items apiece, with me buying Tokyo a nice hand bag and a jacket. We headed to the food court when Rick Rick tapped my shoulder, I looked behind me and notice two bad bitches following us. One of them had a lil boy with her. We made it to the food court and ordered our food. As we ate, I peeped them sneaking glances at us. Rick Rick had this goofy ass smirk on his face. I looked at him and then turned my head to look at the shorty he was looking at, I had to admit, she was bad as fuck.

"You like that gang?" I asked Rick Rick.

"She straight," he replied trying to downplay the situation.

"She straight my ass, I see that goofy ass smirk on yo face nigga." He smiled even harder.

"You know what, I'm about to go introduce myself," he smiled. "You funny as hell boi, do you though," he said smiling.

"Shy ass nigga," I joked walking off. I walked up to their table, "sorry to interrupt you all, but me and my brother couldn't help but notice how beautiful you looked sitting over here alone. I didn't want to be rude so, I decided to come over here and introduce myself, I'm Stevo." I extended my hand to the dark skin one first.

"I'm Brandy," she replied.

"And I'm NeNe," the mixed one stated extending her hand.

"NeNe, I thought it couldn't be." I kissed the back of her hand and she blushed. Rick Rick walked up.

"Hi, I'm Brandy." Brandy stated introducing herself. We all hit it off and exchanged numbers with me getting NeNe's number and Rick Rick getting Brandy's. We left the Mall and headed back to the hotel. Rick Rick was driving, we were smoking the exotic weed that we got from King Lando.

"Man, boi I like that bitch gang," Rick Rick stated referring to NeNe. "I can't lie, that mixed bitch bad too, but you know I like my dark skin bitches," he continued.

"I think that's the bitch Gang," I stated.

"What bitch?" he asked. I looked at him a moment, then it's like a light bulb came on in his head. "That bitch name was NeNe wasn't it?" he asked excitedly.

"Yeah, boi," I answered.

"You think it's her?"

"She did have a baby with her, it could be her," I stated. It's only one way to find out," I smiled.

We made it back to the hotel and decided that we were gone check out King Lando'nem club tonight. I had time to kill so, I called NeNe and five minutes into the conversion she told me everything thing I needed to know. As luck would have it, she was indeed the NeNe we were here for.

"So, what you on tonight?" she asked.

"I don't know, I was thinking about sliding to Club Lava tonight," I stated.

"That's the spot, what you know about Club Lava?" she asked.

"Nothing really, honestly, the owner invited us."

"King Lando?" She interrupted, "You know King Lando?" she asks slightly impressed.

"Yes and no, I kind of just met him at the Gucci store."

*'Gucci store,'* she thought.

"What, you know him?" I asked surprised.

"I know of him, who don't know him, that nigga run Atlanta."

*'This shit was easier than I thought it would be this bitch a motor mouth,'* I thought.

"You gotta watch them niggas tho, my baby daddy and his best friend Chase was beefing with them niggas, they sneaky as fuck. Especially, that lil ass boy Delyuntay."

*'So that's what C stand for CHASE, keep talking ma,'* I thought. "So, you don't fuck with yo baby daddy no mo?" I asked.

"Nope, his dead-beat ass, left me and his son to go fuck with his cousin Choppa in Miami," she stated like she was getting mad.

*'Ok they cousins huh that make sense.'* "Don't worry I got you ma."

"You got me?" she flirted. I could hear her smiling through the phone. "Yeah, whatever you need ma, is your rent paid up?" I asked her. "Shit'd, it's like rent come around every week," she laughed.

"Don't trip ma, rent on me these next two months," I stated.

"Really?" she asked. "But you don't even know me?"

"I know, but it's just something about you that I find very valuable, you seem like a woman that deserves the world," I stated.

"Oh, my God, you're a life saver. I mean, I'm not no broke hoe so please don't think that," she replied all ghetto like. "I'm just very appreciative."

I laughed, "it isn't nothing like that ma, I'll just consider it my good deed for the month. I could drop it off to you before I go to the club so I don't forget," I stated in attempt to get her address.

"You sure you not just trying to get no pussy?" she asked.

"Nawl ma, it's something about you," I lied.

"You sure?" she asked skeptically.

"I'm positive baby."

"Okay, I guess I can just send you my address," then she stated, "no funny business Mr. nice guy," she flirted.

"Sounds good, I'm about to shower and I'll call you when I get out!"

"Okay, sounds good and thank you, again," she cooed. Two minutes later she sent me her address. *'Bingo,'* I thought, it matched one of the ones I had. I face timed Rick Rick and updated him on everything.

"You the G.O.A.T. my boi," he laughed, "but on some real shit, let's just see how this shit play out, we got leverage now, we can milk this shit.

"You just like that bitch Brandy," I laughed.

"A lil bit," he smiled. "Now we got one up on them niggas," he stated. I called Flo and told him everything.

"Perfect mane, stay on point and keep that bitch in eyesight, we about to put some pressure on these niggas," he stated. "We're going to use that bitch and the kid, for leverage."

"Say no mo," I responded, "we were just thinking the same thing," I stated before hanging up.

I called NeNe back, she picked up on the first ring. "Aye ma, send me your cash app and we just gone link up for breakfast or something."

"Okay, I'm about to do it now, but thank you, so very much," she stated.

"It's all good," I replied. I sent her three-thousand dollars through one of the bogus cash apps I had connected to my iPhone; she texted me back a heart emoji. I just smiled, cash ruled the world.

We got dressed and headed out to the club. We got there and called the number that was on the card. King Lando picked up on the first ring.

"Who this?" he asked screaming over the loud music.

"This Stevo, we met in the Gucci store."

"Awe yeah, my Chicago niggas… where y'all at?"

"I'm outside your spot, but this line long as shit," I stated.

"Don't trip, I'm about to send lil bruh to come and get you mane, stay put."

We were standing to the side just chilling admiring all the bad bitches when Delyuntay walked up with the same nigga he was with in the Gucci store. This lil nigga was most definitely on some grown man shit, he was definitely in his bag, he had on his chains and shit, he definitely looked like money. He was laughing at something that the nigga he was with said. We were smoking when they walked up.

"I see y'all made it mane," Delyuntay stated shaking our hands, "this my cousin Antonio."

"What's up mane, welcome to the A," he stated.

"It feels good to be here Joe, especially with all these fine ass bitches around, damn this must be the bad bitch capital," I joked.

Antonio sparked up a blunt himself, "I might as well get my smoke on too," he smiled.

"Delyuntay!" Some petite sexy ass brown skin chick hollered.

"Layah, what the fuck are you doing here?"

"Nigga, you not my daddy, I'm your big sister, and last time I checked I was 22," she smirked. She was with another chick, they both had on little bitty ass dresses. "You gone introduce me to your friends?" Layah asked. "This Stevo and Rick Rick, my niggas from Chi-Raq," he bragged.

"I'm Layah, and this my friend China," she stated looking me in the eyes the whole time. I licked my lips… she did to

"Nice to meet you ma," I stated.

"Nice to meet you to pa," she flirted. "Let me hit that Tonio," Layah asked and he passed her the weed.

"You lucky you're my cousin because I don't be smoking after chicks out here," he joked passing her the weed.

"Don't play with me punk," she joked punching him in the arm.

While they were busy talking, I was paying attention to this charger, it actually looked like a Hellcat, that muthafucka was creeping up with its lights off. I reached for my F&N and looked at Rick Rick and he was already on point. The Hellcat sped up and made it to us within 6 seconds. A nigga was hanging out the roof with a choppa and he began letting that bitch off. Everybody ducked but Rick Rick, because Rick Rick was on his ass, he had the Glocks out bussing them bitches. I dived on Layah and covered her with my body. I don't know what made me do it but I did.

Delyuntay took cover, he must not have a weapon on him because he wasn't shooting back. I rolled onto my back and began letting shots off.

*'Damn, these niggas gangsters…'* Delyuntay thought. Rick Rick must have hit the driver because the car crashed into the curb. I jumped up and me and Rick Rick began shooting the car up. Once we felt it was safe enough to proceed we ran over to the car, the driver was slumped and the other nigga was leaking, we emptied our clips into them.

"Bitch ass niggas," I stated. We looked up and saw King Lando'nem running up with their weapons drawn. They looked at us with admiration.

"Thanks," King Lando spoke as they walked over to the car next to us.

"Guess who it is?" One of King Lando's henchmen asked.

"Who?" asked King Lando.

"T-MAC," the henchmen stated.

King Lando smiled, "finally got his bitch ass huh?"

"You know this was a hit, right?" the henchman asked.

"Yeah, it's on now," King Lando stated.

All the sudden Layah screamed, "Oh, my God nooooo!!!" We all ran over to her and on the floor next to her dead, was no other than her cousin Antonio. His eyes were open and blood was coming out of his mouth, and half of his head was missing from the impact of the assault rifle.

"We have to go, he gone sis, the police coming," Delyuntay stated.

"No, I'm not leaving him."

"Y'all get out of here," King Lando urged, "imma call y'all," he stated giving both me and Rick Rick a pound. We were turning to leave when King Lando grabbed my arm, "Thanks, for saving my sister and brother's life, I owe y'all mane."

"It wasn't nothing, but we gotta slide, I'll call you Joe." And just like that we were gone.

# Chapter (15)
## - Tiffany -

**I** was sitting at the kitchen table in total disbelief, I'd just turned off the local news. I couldn't believe that Jockey was dead. The news said that she was found with half of her face blown off and her tongue cut out. She was found by some fisher man floating in the river. I couldn't think of who would want to do some shit like this to her. She didn't have any known beef plus, she was from Atlanta. I was even more surprise at how Kiesha reacted to the news. I called her to send my condolences and to my surprise she replied, "Damn, she must have pissed somebody off."

I was in utter shock, I mean they were close. I guess Kiesha is way more savage then I give her credit for. I already had a banging ass headache from the conversation I had with Choppa last night. This nigga had the nerves to ask me to set the DIME-BOYZ up, talking about they robbed him and he wanted me to prove my loyalty and shit. Nigga, I'm the one that got yo stupid ass robbed and the nigga that you riding around with is the one who did it; but of course, I will never tell him that. That nigga doesn't have any value especially, when I be putting this good stuff on him.

I played my role tho, because a wise bitch once told me don't nothing beat the double cross like the triple cross. For some reason, I had a feeling Chase was geeking shit up and misleading Choppa. That's why I couldn't fuck with Choppa like that, he way to gullible to be a street nigga. I had the perfect nigga to vent to yup, Valo. I just loved his fine chocolate ass. Outta all the DIME-BOYZ, I fucked with Valo the most, plus, he owed me some dick. Yeah, yeah, yeah, I know that's my sister man, but ever since I got a taste of that big ass dick I've been hooked, and this presented the perfect opportunity to finished what we started.

I called Ja'Valo and he didn't answer, I called him again and he picked up on the last ring.

"What's up shawty?"

"Where you at?" I asked him. "Where I'm at?" he answered.

"Yeah, I got some shit I need to tell you asap."

"Okay, speak on it."

"Not over the phone tho."

"Okay, I'm at the pub shooting pool, ride down on me."

"Can we meet somewhere private?"

He paused, "um yeah, meet me at the Low."

"Okay, cool," I responded. The Low was the block the DIME-BOYZ took from Baby and Mula.

I pulled up and the block was full as usual, a lotta young niggas out hustling packs for the DIME-BOYZ.

"What's up Tiffany?" Jason, one of the DIME-BOYZ block captains asked me as I made it to the front door. He was standing there like a body guard.

"Sup Jason," I responded uninterested, trying to walk pass him.

"Where you going mane?"

"Inside, to see Valo, and I would appreciate if you will move yo big ass out the way." He stepped up to me, and he was every bit of 6'8, 320lbs solid.

"You got a smart-ass mouth bitch!"

"Bitch? Un un, I got your bitch," I said reaching in my bag for my lady .380, even tho I never used it before I was ready to shoot this nigga.

"Yo, chill Jay," Smooth spoke up, "she here to see Valo, I got the call ten minutes ago." He looked at Smooth and then at me.

"Well, this bitch better learns some manners because one day the shoe might be back on the other foot," he replied with hate in his heart.

I looked at smooth, "thank you," I mouthed before walking past Jason fat ugly ass. I made it to the top floor where Valo was at. He was sitting on the sofa looking good enough to eat. I don't know what it is that he does to me, but I just love his chocolate skin, long dreads, and white teeth. He's tall so that's a plus too.

"So, what's up ma? Are you just going to stare at me, or are you gone tell me what was so important that you couldn't tell me over the phone?"

I blushed in embarrassment, but I managed to smile. "Boy, don't do too much," I flirted. He had on his wife beater and his body was in great shape. He had his DIME-BOYZ chain on, with some type of jogging shorts looking like a ghetto celebrity. I couldn't help myself from looking at his dick print. I sat down on the sofa beside him. He lit up a blunt and I told him the plot that Choppa came up with to take out him and his crew.

He just looked at me for a minute after I ran the whole story down to him. At first, I didn't know if he believed me or not, but then he spoke.

"Why are you telling me this shit?" he asked.

"Why am I telling you this? Why wouldn't I tell you some shit this important?"

"I mean, Choppa is your man and shit ma," he stated.

"Yeah, but he doesn't put food in my mouth, only dick. You niggas put food in my mouth, y'all niggas feeds me and my sisters, and I never bite the hands that feeds me," I replied licking my lips. I could tell that the weed was having an effect on him because he was looking at me with low seductive eyes. He also couldn't stop licking his lips. I don't know what made me do it, but I went in for a kiss; I was inches away from his mouth when he moved his head back, and grabbed the back of my neck shoveling it towards his dick. I love a man that could take charge, and I loved sucking his dick, especially.

I love the power it gave me over him. I didn't waste no time, I pulled down his shorts and his boxer briefs. His dick popped out, he threw a pillow off the sofa in between his legs and motioned for me to get on the floor between his legs. I quickly complied, I couldn't wait to taste that dick again. I palmed his dick and lick it from the base to the tip. I made sure I paid special attention to the bottom of his dick head. I slowly began engulfing his dick in my mouth until it hit the back of my throat. I slowly began sucking his dick up and down. Slobber was beginning to drip down the side of his dick.

I knew he liked it sloppy, so I made shit, I put extra spit on his dick. My head skills caused him to grab the back of my head and push the remaining of his dick in my throat. I almost gaged.

"Yeah, ma, suck that dick ma," he moaned. "Look at me when you suck this dick."

I opened my throat and did my best impression of supper head. My eyes were starting to water but I didn't stop my rhythm. I made sure that dick was sloppy wet and I used both of my hands to jag it while I sucked the head. I slowed down because I felt his dick pulse jumping like he was about to cum.

"Damn, ma, you give the best fucking head ever. Please don't stop."

I just looked up at him with his dick in my mouth. Him begging me not to stop had my pussy gushing wet, I was throbbing and I wanted some dick now. I love the power I had over men with my wet mouth. I kissed his dick head and stood up. I had on a cute sundress with a tong on. I straddled him and be popped one of my titties out. Both my nipples were pierce, which I could tell he liked because I felt his dick jumped as he sucked on them. I was sitting on his dick and I could feel the heat from his dick on my cat through my tongs.

I reached under him and pulled my tong aside, and before he could protest I was sliding my wet tight pussy on his dick. I slid down inch by inch until I was totally impaled.

"Oh, my God," he moaned.

I slowly began riding his dick.

"Fuck me!" Valo I moaned as I was kissing his neck.

This nigga had my legs shaking, I mean he was so much larger then Choppa and I felt every inch as he was hitting spots I didn't even know exist. My eyes rolled to the back of my head, "that's my spot...... I'm.... cumming...... on...... your dick Valo, I can feel it.......in my stomach."

"Yeah, ma.... cum on my dick...." he moans cockily slamming me down into his lap.

I was riding the shit out of his dick, I had both of my feet planted down on the sofa as I hovered over him. I began convulsing like I was having a seizure. He picked me up off of him and bent me over the sofa. I knew he just wanted to see my fat ass jiggle in the air as he hit it, but I wasn't complaining because I was loving every minute of it, and doggy was one of my favorite position. He eased back into my pussy from the back and began pounding me out.

"Who.... pussy.... is this?" he barked.

"Yours.... daddddddy........ it's yours...... you can have it," I moaned. "Beat this pussy up....... I been a bad girl......"

He began beating my pussy up. He then used the juices pooled at the base of his dick as lubricant, as he eased a finger in my ass hole. My pussy instantly got wetter and I began cumming once again. My hot fluids were too much for him because he announced that he was cumming too.

"I'm cumming......"

I felt his hot seeds blasting off inside of me. And once he was done, I turned around and sat on the sofa as he stood in front of me. And then I cleaned his dick off with my mouth. I loved the taste of my own juices. "I think that's was the best dick I've ever had, it was definitely worth the wait," I stated honestly.

"Smart girl," he smiled.

*'My sister gone have go share that dick,'* I thought.

We cleaned ourselves off and got dressed. I was heading out the door but stopped in my tracks. "So, what are we going to do about that situation?" I asked him. That dick was so good I was ready to kill for this nigga. *'It's crazy what good dick could do to a bitch,'* I thought.

"Don't trip ma, I'll keep you posted. We already got a cake baked for his ass. See, he got a cousin named Chase...."

*'Hearing him say Chase's name made my heart skip a beat, how the fuck he knows about Chase?'* I thought.

"See, the nigga Chase," he continued, "Robbed Prince the other day."

*'Robbed Prince?'* I thought. *'What the fuck, I told him that the DIME BOYZ was off limits!'*

"He didn't really get shit, but off that move alone he dead," Valo stated. "Choppa gone get it to, and the other niggas they with."

"Damn, that's fucked up. Is Prince straight?" I asked.

"Yeah, he a gangsta so he cool, but we can't let that shit go for nothing."

"I feel you," I replied, but the inside of my mind was going crazy. I was putting two and two together... *'Chased robbed Choppa and told him it was Prince. Chase robbed Prince and told Choppa that Prince'nem tried to rob him. This nigga doing too much,'* I thought. *'I can't wait to call his shiesty ass because he fucking my money up.'*

Valo came up with a master plan and I promised to play my part. I left immediately after the plan was made. I made it home and took a hot shower, and after I took my shower I jumped in my bed. My air conditioner had my house nice and cool. I loved my new house, and most importantly, only my sisters knew where I lived. I closed my blinds and laid in bed, it was midday but that dick had me sleepy, and before I knew it I drifted off to sleep....

* * *

## - Kiesha -

**I** heard that when you kill somebody, you have nightmares and shit, or you'll be paranoid all the time but not me, I felt good. I felt like a new woman. I felt like I could take over the world. I felt like God, taking a life made me feel like I had the power of God. I was ready to pop off if a bitch or nigga even looked at me wrong. Lowkey tho, that gangsta shit made my pussy wet as fuck. When I killed Jockey, I went home and played with my pussy. I knew that all the DIME-BOYZ was surprised at how gangsta I was, and it was like a high to me to be viewed so powerful.

I was driving in my new Audi A8, that I got from Flo, it was the white one he loved so much with the red insides. He said it was for me being so loyal. I pulled up at Dee Dee's house and blew the horn; she called me and asked could I go get my nails done with her. I jumped to the opportunity, I thought she was sexy. I was also into girls yes, I'm bisexual. Especially, girls that's just founding out their beautiful. She walked out the house, she had on some tight jeans and a tight shirt that showed off her curves. She hopped in.

"I thought you was Flo ma," she stated, "he letting you drive his whip and shit, no?" she asked surprised.

"Naw he gave me this," I replied showing her the title.

"Damn, ma, you must got some good ass pussy," she said sounding just like them niggas.

She might have looked all girly and shit, but she still sounded like a nigga, just with a soft voice.

"Naw, it's not that type of party," I clarified, "he say it was for my loyalty."

"Awe okay," she smiled.

We pulled up to the nail shop and was met at the door by a small Asian woman. We got our feet and nails done, and we were in and out, thank God. I still hated the smell of nail polish. We rode around and chopped it up. Dee Dee proved to have a good heart under that hard exterior she displayed. We were on the west side when we ran out of blunts and Dee Dee asked me to stop at the gas station to get some. I volunteered to go in the gas station. I walked in and was greeted by an Arab muthafucka giving me the googly eyes and shit. I mugged his ass and ordered my blunts and got a juice for me and Dee Dee. I also, told the dude to put $40 on my pump and he did.

Dee Dee was already out the car pumping the gas when I came out. We were laughing and joking about something when I saw her eyes go big as shit, and then I felt the cold steel to the back of my neck.

"Bitch don't move," the deep voice demanded.

I was frozen in fear. Within seconds, we were surrounded by mask men. I saw them put a black bag over Dee Dee head before they put one on over mines. Next, thing you know we were thrown in some sort of sprinter van. I could hear them saying that they only needed one of us. I tried to resist, but I was hit with something on the back of the head and was knocked out cold.

"The gas station man called the police, then that's when I woke up in the hospital," I stated. Appreciating the gang letting me speak without being interrupted.

"Try to remember anything else you might have missed," Valo stated.

"I heard them say Dee Dee name and something about a ransom."

"Can you remember anything else?" Flo asked.

I was surrounded by the whole gang laying in the hospital bed, with minor cuts and bruises to my body. I was waiting for the doctor to discharge me.

"Did you hear any names, think…" Valo demanded.

"Yeah, I heard one name," I replied.

"What name was that?" Ondat asked impatient.

"Hitman" I replied……

# Chapter (16)
# - Baby -

*'T*oday might turn out to be a good ass day,' I thought, as I was sitting at the kitchen table rolling up a blunt in my hideaway spot. I've been laying low since the DIME-BOYZ put that play down killing all my people, but patients are a virtual. Now look, the tables have turned, we really caught the first lady slipping, them muthafuckas thought they couldn't be touched, lil cocky fuckers. We had her ass tied up in the basement in her underwear freezing her ass off. I felt like since we were going to wipe they whole fucking crew out, we might as well get some money out this shit. *'I wonder what was the going rate for the first lady,'* I smiled at the thought.

It wasn't gone take me long to find out tho. I had already taken pictures of Dee Dee chained up in the basement in her underwear. I also, took a picture with my mask on with her DIME-GIRL chain on. See, I did my research on them niggas, and I was so surprised at how much money they ass was making off my muthafucking block. I'm thankful for that nigga Hitman, he gone go far places. See, when I was on top, I did business with them Choppa city niggas and we always kept things one thousand with each other.

My favorite cousin Kayla stayed in the Bay, (Tampa Bay.) I grabbed my burner phone and organized the pictures, I then sent them to Flo phone with a message that read... IF YOU WANT TO SEE YOUR DIAMOND GIRL EVER AGAIN I NEED 10 BRICKS OF THAT RAW AND 500,000 CASH IN 48 HOURS OR THE BITCH IS GOOD AS DEAD. I was still waiting on a reply. Hitman came down here with Rico, Flocka, and Rocko my Choppa city niggas. I fucked with all these niggas, it's nothing to come together when you got a common enemy.

This nigga Rocko was a pussy hound tho, he done already tricked off with one of the crack head bitches name Lea that Choppa gave him. His personal dick eater is what Choppa called her. These Choppa city niggas was different tho, they shoot first and ask questions later and that's what I liked about them. I didn't really like that nigga Choppa tho, he was soft to me plus, I think he knew I smashed his bitch Tiffany. I couldn't wait to be back on top. I wish I knew were they was getting they dope from, but it is what it is. Overall tho, I was ready to get my blocks back. I had my partner Jason ears open to everything. These stupid muthafuckas made him the block Captain, like I said, lil cocky fuckers.

They must have forgot who the fuck fed them lil niggas on my block, ME that's who. A lotta them niggas switched up, but Jason played both sides and reported everything to me. We came up with a move that was gone fuck them people up. We were planning to hitting their block up in broad daylight. I knew how they got down and I was not impressed, they killed a bunch of lil niggas. I can't lie tho, they took a lot of real niggas from me so I don't know what made them think that I wasn't gone get any get back. I was actually excited.

About an hour later, we were all together in the spot. I called Hitman and we decided to come together on this hit. We all had our different reasons. I didn't trust these niggas from Atlanta. Especially, this nigga Chase, the eyes don't lie, that muthafucka was up to something and I made a mental note to keep a close eye on him. We still haven't fed the bitch since we snatched her ass up. I know she was down there freezing because it was cool as hell in that basement. I have to give it to her tho, that lil bitch took all that shit like a G. She wasn't crying or begging, nor would she tell us where they were getting their dope from, which kinda bothered me a lil bit, but I shook it off as being paranoid.

Speaking of this bitch, let me go check on this bitch because Mula been down there with the bitch for like 30 minutes straight. But like I told him, she's worth more to us alive then dead. I excused myself and headed to the basement. *'Damn, it's cool down here,'* I thought as I made it to the bottom step. The basement had two bed rooms in it. One room didn't have shit in it and that's where Dee Dee was chained up at, I could hear a voice coming from the room. I opened up the door and Mula had his dick out pissing on Dee Dee's head, her face was swollen and her lips was bloody.

Once he was done he looked at me and smiled. "What's up B?" he asked shaking his dick off.

"Man, what the fuck…" I asked him heatedly, "what are you doing mane?"

"Nothing," he replied hunching his shoulders.

"Nothing?" I asked, "you fucking up the money mane, I told you to leave that bitch alone because she worth more to us alive."

"Easy for you to say."

"Easy for me to say?" I asked.

"Yeah, nigga, easy for you to say, you're not the one that got stomped out by this bitch and her crew. Besides, I didn't do nothing but ruff her up a lil bit… she'll live," he spat.

"You still a bitch ass nigga," Dee Dee stated weakly. She refused to let the Hot Boyz see her sweat, she felt like she'd rather die on her feet then on her knees.

Mula kicked her in her stomach, "shut up bitch."

She laughed at him, "you kick like a bitch" she stated spitting out blood. I grabbed him by the arm, he tried yanking away but I gripped him tighter.

"What the fuck mane? Keep your head in the game, don't let this bitch get in your head because we have bigger fish to fry."

"Yeah, you right mane," he said looking at Dee Dee with disgust.

We made it back upstairs and I double backed down there and I switched her to the other room with the bed in it and gave her some McDonalds and a blanket. I really didn't have no love for the bitch, but I didn't want to chance her dying on us and we don't get shit. When I made it back upstairs, everybody was amped up and ready for the hit. I knew it was gone be pretty easy because we had an inside man…. Jason.

\* \* \*

## - Ondat -

*I* had a funny feeling about today for some reason, I couldn't shake the feeling that was bubbling in my gut. The whole gang was distraught over Dee Dee being missing especially, with Kiesha fresh out the hospital, shit was definitely tense in the streets. Word had gotten out about Dee Dee getting snatched and that we put up a hundred thousand dollars out for anybody who could provide us with some type of information that could lead us to the niggas responsible for this shit. We had our eyes locked in on Choppa after Tiffany put Valo on game about the lil play he had in stores for us.

Kidnapping wasn't his game tho, he didn't have the balls for no shit like that, but I wasn't gone put shit pass nobody, we were still on his ass. What bothers me the most was nobody we knew ever heard of a Hitman. We didn't even know how the nigga looked or nothing. *'Maybe she heard the wrong name or something,'* I thought. I was chilling on the LOW, that's what we named the block we took from baby. It was just me, Valo, Smooth, Jason, and a couple of the lil niggas. Some plumbers were working on the house next to our trap.

I loved this block, we're doing crazy numbers out this bitch. We had a long night tho, nobody been to sleep since Dee Dee been gone. Flo'nem was still out looking for her, he wanted us to stay on the block so that we could keep our ears to the street. Stevo and Rick Rick was still in the 'A' baking that cake. They both took the news pretty hard about DeeDee and they were ready to come back and paint the city red, but we had to keep that ace in the hole down there.

I was sitting on the stool in front of the building when I spotted crackhead Lea bopping up the street as if she was on a mission. She had her usual seductive walk and she walked right up to me.

"Can I holla at y'all a minute?" she asked me with urgency in her voice.

I stood up, "this betta be good," I mumble. I wasn't in the mood for I owe you and shit. "Speak ma, we all gang," I said pointing to the guys.

"No offense, but I'd rather talk to you and Valo only." We all looked at each other.

"What's up with the secret shit?" Smooth asked her but she didn't say nothing and just looked at him. The others stepped aside.

"So, what's up?" Valo asked her.

"I think I have some information that would be useful for you about Dee Dee," she stated.

"Yeah?" I asked with excitement in my voice. "What you got?" I asked her.

"Okay, I was tricking off with this nigga named Rocko, an out of town nigga that's up here with Choppa'nem, and I overheard him mentioned the DIME-BOYZ."

"What did he say?" I asked as my body begin tensing up.

"And, where are they?" Valo stated.

"They said something about hitting y'all pockets before they kill the bitch, and we were at a hotel on the East side."

"Did he say what bitch he was talking about?" Valo asked.

"No, but my guess was he was talking about Dee Dee."

"Okay, anything else?" I asked. She looked at the ground. I grabbed her chin to pick her head up, she looked me in her eyes and I can see the fear in them. "Speak ma."

She hesitated a minute then she spoke, "he also said wiping y'all out was going to be easy because they had an inside man in y'all organization."

My nose flared, "fuck you mean ma?" I asked stepping closer to her.

"That's what he said," she responded visibly shaken.

"He was just talking freely like that in front of you?" Valo asked confused.

"I was doing my thang on him while he was on the phone," she said referring to sucking his dick.

"Thanks ma," I replied giving her a hand full of work.

"Thanks, but I didn't do it for this, I did it because y'all always treat me nice and with respect, and y'all Sasha's kids. She still my girl," she stated but still shoveling the drugs in her pockets.

"Thanks," I replied. "Did you hear who he was on the phone with?" I asked her. She looked in the sky as if she was trying to remember, then it hit her; she remembered.

"Some nigga name Hitman," she responded. We both looked at each other.

"What name you say ma?" Valo asked.

"Hitman," she responded confidently.

"Thanks," we both replied.

Valo called Flo and updated him on everything. I was on the phone when I noticed a blue Ford F150 creeping down the block. At first, I thought it was the police until I seen a nigga with gold in his mouth driving. I kept my eyes on the truck as it rode pass me without the driver even looking my way.

*'They say happiness is one of God's greatest gifts. Without that you're missing your blessing's.*

I don't know what made me think of that, but it all happened so fast. Two niggas lifted up from inside the flat bed of the F150 with two hand guns apiece. Before I could even say anything Valo was on they ass.

We all had 30 shot Glocks with the switch on them, which made our hand guns shoot like the Ak47. Valo aimed his gun and began to gunning the men down. Smooth followed suit. I couldn't even reach for my shit because I was pinned behind a car so I took cover. Valo, Smooth, and Jason was behind the car next to me shooting and taking cover at the same time. I heard some shots coming from behind me and then I felt a hot sensation in my leg.

I looked back and the guys that pretended to be plumbers all had guns out shooting our way. *'Fuck...'* I thought. Another truck pulled up from down the block and jumped out with choppas bucking our way to. I wondered was this how it felt in Iraq during the war. I slid all the way under the car I was taking cover behind. My arm and leg were on fire, I'm shot in both places. I heard Jason tell Smooth to run and that he was gone cover him. Two of our lil niggas was laid out in the street dead. One of them dropped right by me while I was under the car.

I will never forget the empty look he had in his eyes as I watch him take his last breath, he was only 16. I saw my lil nigga Treal shooting at the niggas from his bed room window, he stayed across the street from the trap house. I don't know how he got a gun because he was only 15, but I admired his braveness. Smooth ran from behind the car expecting Jason to cover him but he didn't, but Valo did and Smooth almost made it to the building but was chopped down by Hitman's AR-15. I finally was able to get my gun out. From under the car I could still see Valo and Jason, I don't know where Valo was getting all this ammunition from but he reloaded and was on they ass again.

It seems like he was the only one shooting back. I saw one of the men stand over Smooth and point a gun in his face, in attempt to finish him off, but I couldn't go for that and pointed my gun from under the car and just began shooting wildly getting a lucky shot off. Hitting him in the head and killing him instantly. Valo was finally outta ammunition. I heard him tell Jason to cover him and that he just needed to make it to the building. I was beginning to fade in and out because now I've lost so much blood.

Jason was behind Valo so Valo couldn't see the look that Jason was giving him; I immediately knew something wasn't right. I used all my might and rolled from under the car. Valo made a run for it and it was like slow motion, nobody was covering him so I began to shoot wildly at our perpetrators to try and cover Valo. Valo almost made it to the door but I watch in horror as Jason aimed his gun at Valo and began emptying his clip on him. I saw Valo's body jerk as I watched one of my best friends fall at the hands of one of our own guys.

A tear escaped my eye. I screamed. I heard police siren and I began crawling towards Valo. I was a bloody mess, I felt a bullet rip through my shoulder blade as I ignored the pain and kept crawling. I had to get to my homie, I saw a guy running up on me outta the corner of my eye.

"Hitman come on..." I heard Jason yell.

*'Hold on, did this nigga just say Hitman.?!* I made it to Valo and I just covered him with my body. I was ready to die with my homie. I couldn't feel a thing in my body. The dude called Hitman walked up to me with his mask off. He was a skinny dark skin nigga with a low cut and black lips. Nothing like the Hitman I imagined. I looked him in the eyes as he smiled and then pumped two shots into my chest, that's when everything went black...

# Chapter (17)
## - Choppa -

"**S**hit. I'm hit, man!" Rico coughed. I looked over at him and notice he was bleeding from the chest.

"Flocka, put some pressure on the wound," I demanded. I was speeding on the interstate looking out for cops while trying to get my mans to the hospital; and get away from a murder scene at the same damn time.

"Hold on man." I heard Flocka pleading.

"Fuck... them fuck niggas had switches on their guns," Flocka yelled.

"Speed this bitch up mane he losing a lotta blood..." Rico eyes began rolling to the back of his head. "Hang on bruh we're almost there," Flocka cried sensing his best friend life slipping away. Rico tried to speak but coughed up blood and began shaking.

"Oh, shit!" I spat. Moments later he went stiff, losing the fight.

"Damn, man fuck," Flocka cried, "he gone bruh! I can't believe a little ass kid kilt my man. Lil nigga was shooting out the window of that fucking house, we definitely have to revisit that muthafucka. Slick muthafuckas, now we lost one of our own," Flocka cried.

We pulled up to the spot and was met by the other cars we had with us. Everybody was fucked up about the loss of Rico, but I was the most. Mostly, because I was the one that sent for him. I knew he had a two-year-old son and I vowed to pay for all of his funeral expenses and take care of his family.

After we watched the news, we learned that we dropped five of them niggas, but what shocked us the most was that, they were claiming that Michael Allison AKA Smooth, was a F.B.I Confidential Informant in an ongoing investigation. I didn't know the nigga Smooth, and I was glad that I never did business with the nigga. But on the other hand, Baby, Mula, and Jason was sweating bullets, after all, Baby was the one who put Smooth in the dope game.

*'Ain't no telling how much he done told them people, this shit definitely changed the game plan. I really gotta get the fuck out of here, Tampa Bay here I come,'* Baby thought. It was all agreed that we would lay low and that we would keep the girl alive for leverage.

\* \* \*

**F**lo was pacing back and forward in the E.R. waiting on the verdict of his Family. His heart was heavy and he felt like he couldn't breathe. He was ready to paint the city red.

"Not my brothers."

That's all he could think of, that, and the fact that them niggas still had Dee Dee doing only God knows what to her. *'Our Family falling apart, everything's fucked up... were the fuck is Prince?'* he thought. He was barely stable, he still couldn't get ahold of Stevo and Rick Rick, they were unaware of everything that was going on. Flo, Kiesha, Tiffany, and Jade was all there in the emergency room with tears falling like the river. The clouds were getting darker and darker by the moment, you could smell the rain in the air.

Jade, tired of sitting around walked up to the receptionist who gave her a dirty look. "What's taking so long?" Jade asked hasty. The skinny blond looks at her with a set of deep blue eyes.

"M'am, like I told you before, the doctors are working around the clock on your family. Unfortunately, we don't have any updates at this moment."

"Bitch please, I don't give no fuck about none of that shit! I want to see my man…" Jade yell knocking over the paperwork that was on the counter drawing the attention of the hospital security.

"Everything okay?" He asked walking up, he was a tall black man with a low haircut and a big head.

"Get the fuck away from me," Jade screamed.

"Woah, woah, woah, clam down miss, I'm just here to help," he responded.

Tiffany walked up and grabbed her sister in a tight bear hug to help clam her down. She knew her sister was madly in love with Ja'Valo and she felt bad for betraying her by having sex with him, but she couldn't help her new-found feelings she'd developed for Valo, especially after his new-found fame and fortune. She also was heartbroken that he may be dead.

"God please give him another chance, I promise I'll be better. I can't do this by myself…" Jade pleaded with God. Tiffany and her sister were pleading with God with the exact same prayer only difference was, she just learned that she was pregnant by Ja'Valo, shit was definitely about to get interesting.

Two doctors walked in and they all rushed over to them. They both had this sad look in their eye and Flo instantly knew something was wrong.

"Doc, what's going on?" Flo spoke up.

"Hi, I'm Dr. Ruby Griffin, and this is Dr. Johnson," the nice-looking older lady spat greeting us.

"What's up with my brother Doc?" Flo interrupted. There was a pregnant pause, and a sad look over came the doctors.

"I'm sorry, there's no easy way to tell you this but we did everything that we could do, but he didn't make it." It was like the whole world froze. Tiffany fainted, "nooooo." Kiesha broke down. Flo screamed, *'this shit can't be happening,'* he thought. He felt like he was having an out of body experience. He stormed out of the emergency room not really aware of what he was doing.

"What do you mean he didn't make it?"

"Sorry m'am," Dr. Ruby offer.

"It's okay," Jade responded with tears in her eyes. She cried as the nurses helped Tiffany up and checking her vitals. Kiesha began screaming hysterically, she was having a panic attack. The nurses tried to calm her down, the E.R. was in complete chaos.

"I just want to see him Doc. I just need to see him one last time please!" Jade pleaded. Dr. Ruby looked her in the eyes and felt sympathy for the young girl. She knew it was against the rules due to the fact that the victim died on the operating room and wasn't patched up properly yet, but she felt due to the circumstances it wouldn't hurt to bend the rules a little. Plus, Jade reminded her of a daughter she never had.

"Okay, listen, I could get in trouble for this but I feel your pain, follow me." Jade followed her to the operating door.

"I will give you five minutes," Dr. Ruby stated.

Jade took a deep breath and said a quick prayer, "God please make me strong, please help me through this," she stated and then proceeded into the room. For some reason the room felt cold and Jade instantly thought that Valo must be freezing, but quickly disregarded the thought. His body was covered up so she slowly walked over to the slab collecting her thoughts. She took another deep breath and slowly pulled the sheet back revealing his face. What she saw caused her to back up and fall to the ground knocking over some of the operating equipment.

Dr. Ruby rushed in, "everything okay child?" she asked with a worried look on her face. Jade tried hard to catch her breath, "breathe child, breathe," the Doc ordered. "What's the matter?" Jade looked at her with wide eyes, she couldn't get the look of the lifeless eyes that she saw so often starring back at her.

"I know this isn't easy child," Dr. Ruby offer trying to console her.

"That's not him!" Jade blurted.

"What?" Dr. Ruby asked walking to his bed to look at the paper work.

"This is him child, the paper work says it, see, look the name is right here, Michael Allison."

"No, that's not him, that's his friend Smooth," Jade stated out of breath. "His name is Ja'Valo Fearis. He's tall, dark skin with long dreads."

Dr. Ruby thought for a minute, "there's one more victim that came in here, but he's in the operating room on the fourth floor. He's the only one hanging on to dear life out of the four that came in; the rest was DOA, except for these two. I must warn you though, he's also in bad shape but he's alive for now."

Jade jumped for joy. "Doc, can you please take me to him? I need to see him."

"Come on child, I can take you to his floor, but they are working on him so they won't let you see him right away. I'm not promising you that you will be able to see him, but last I've heard is he's alive."

Jade jumped for joy, "come on take me please," she yelled pulling Dr. Ruby's arm.

\* \* \*

**F**lo was walking through the lobby with his head down and the tears wouldn't stop flowing. All he wanted to do was kill. Kill, kill, kill… He still felt like this was all a bad dream. He was sad that the person that was dead was his twin brother and his child hood friend Ondat. His soul wouldn't accept that his brothers was gone. He was so distraught that he couldn't think straight. He made it outside the hospital and lit his blunt, he needed to smoke, the exotic weed burned his lungs causing him to cough.

Once inside the car he grabbed the fifth of Remy that he was drinking and took three big gulps, the burning sensation didn't affect him at all, he actually welcomed it. He wanted to numb the pain which was unbearable. He tried to phone Prince, "damn it," he shouted slamming his phone forcefully on the floor panel when Prince's phone went to the voice mail. *'I hope he okay,'* he thought. He grabbed his 30 shot Glock out of the glove department and sped down the interstate.

He made it to the Low in record time, he was surprise at how much traffic was still flowing. "Why the fuck these muthafuckas not hunting? These bitch ass niggas kilt my brother," he stated harshly talking to himself. He ran up in the building that Jason was in charge of and used his key to unlock the door. Seeing Valo's shirt almost broke him down but he kept his composure. He went to the back room and lifted the floor boards where a safe was located underneath, he punched in the combination and the safe opened. His mouth dropped once he noticed it was empty.

"Ahhhhh…" he yelled knocking over everything that was on the dresser counter. He was beyond heated. He had about 12 bricks and 1.1 million dollars unaccounted for, and Jason and Prince was missing. Not to mention that the money that was missing out of the safe was put aside to pay Veronica for the last shipment. She was expecting that money in two days. *'Me, Prince, and Valo was the only ones that knew the code to this muthafucka,'* he thought. He searched the house up and down and came up empty handed. He felt like his whole life was falling apart.

He jumped back into the car and headed to the headquarters. He pulled up and scanned the block. The traffic was still moving but he only had about a kilo of work out here which wasn't nothing for him after he paid his workers, he would net around fifty grand. *'It must be my fucking lucky day,'* he thought jumping out the car with his gun out. Lil Discount was serving a tall skinny nigga that went by the name of Pimping Paul. He felt like baby was pure pussy for letting niggas take his block so he was loyal to the **DIME-BOYZ** and liked how they moved. Seeing the look on his face Lil Discount straightened out his posture but became very uncomfortable.

"Sup big homie, you cool?" he asked.

"Yeah, I'm cool," Flo responded giving him his signature smile.

"Whatever you need big homie I'm on it, real shit," he volunteered flashing his 40glock.

"For show," Flo responded. "Yo, Pimping let me holla at you for a minute."

"Who me?" Paul asked pointing to himself.

"Who else name Pimping nigga?" Flo asked getting more heated.

"What's up mane?" he asked walking slowly up to Flo.

"You seen your nephew lately?"

"Who, Jason?" he asked confused.

"Yeah, you heard from him lately?"

"Naw man, I haven't seen him in weeks."

"Awe okay," Flo replied pretending that he was about to walk off. He suddenly stopped in his tracks, "damn, I left my phone in the crib." Seeing Paul with his phone in his hand he looked at him. "Pimping let me use yo phone really quick?" he asked Paul.

"My shit about to die youngan," he spat.

"Don't worry, I'll be quick," Flo insisted. Paul hesitantly handed his phone over. Flo went right into his call history. He saw Jason's name nine times in the last hour.

*'This muthafucka want to lie to me!'* Flo thought. He looked at Jason's number and press send, Jason picked up on the first ring.

"Yo unc, what's good, did you scope out Flo men block yet? How many niggas out there we ready to take'em out?" Flo hung up the phone.

"You niggas think shit sweet?" Flo asked. Lil Discount just stood with his mouth wide open.

"So, you over here scoping out our block huh bitch nigga?" Lil Discount asked getting heated.

"Look man, I can explain," Pimping Paul stutter.

"Explain that shit to these 30 shots," Lil Discount responded shooting Paul in his face, as a chunk of his brain flew to the wall.

Flo began firing shots in Paul's chest and stomach. The block was simi full but once people heard them shots everybody scattered. They shot Paul a combine sixty times, clearly over killing him. They both took off in different directions with Flo jumping in his ride and smashing off. He pulled up to his hide out spot that only Valo knew about. Walking in the house made him feel even worse. He showered, burned his clothes, changed guns, and change clothes.

He sat down and began texting Jason, he had a master plan. He knew he needed that money or work back, Flo had a funny feeling that Jason did more than just take the money. He had a feeling that Jason back doored Ondat, Valo, and Smooth, his gut was telling him so. After all, he was one of Baby and Mula guys. The more he thought about it the more it made sense to him.

"Y'all muthafuckas want to play, let's play," he said to himself using his spare cell phone to call Kill and Shootsum....

"Yo," Shootsum answered on the first ring.

"Yo, this Flo, I need y'all bruh."

"Everything okay?" Shootsum asked.

"Nawl mane, shit all fucked up, muthafuckas kilt my brothers," he cried.

"What you just say dog?" he asked angrily.

"Yeah, bruh, read the address I just sent you and meet me there in an hour."

"I'm on my way," they replied hanging up the phone.

*'Shit about to get real,'* Flo thought, it's on. He texted Jason pretending he was Paul. Jason text back immediately. Flo smiled his signature smile. "Game Time…"

# Chapter (18)

**P**rince sat in the interrogation room handcuff to the desk. He still had on his street clothes but was stripped of his jewelry, cell phone, shoe laces, and money. He'd been sitting uncomfortably for the last thirteen hours and was freezing cold. He'd actually dosed off a time or two, he lost the track of time and the rumbling in his stomach indicated how hungry he was. He had no idea of the massacre that took place on his guys. One thing was for certain, Prince name held weight in the streets of Miami, it put fear in a lot of people hearts. He was actually the hood favorite, that was a part of the reason he was in this sticky situation now.

He thought back to the thirteen hours prior to before he got locked up. Prince pulled out of his drive way in his midnight blue B.M.W. headed out to talk to the streets, he was looking for Dee Dee high and low. He knew that since the police wasn't involved that his best bet was to talk to the streets. He stopped at the neighborhood store to talk to Omar who welcomed him to the back so they could chat privately in his office.

"Omar, I'm losing it OG, Dee Dee missing and Flo just called me to tell me some nigga name Hitman was the one responsible for snatching her up. Baby demanding a Ransom sending pics and shit, I'm ready to kill everything in sight," Lil Prince expressed stressfully.

"I understand fully young blood and I have been on it too, with that being said, I have some info on this Hitman character," Omar stated.

"You do?" Prince asked raising an eye brow.

"From what I've learned, he's a part of this clique that goes by the name of Choppa City. A bunch of ruthless niggas that's known for shooting shit up with choppas. Word is that, Hitman is an actual hit man, him and his little brother did a lotta work for a lotta heavy hittas around the state. They were considered the best two-man group that got shit done fast and reliable. That was until they took a job to take out Ramirez, one of Sasha's old friends. See, I knew Ramirez and I liked the way him, Sasha, Rambo, and George ran shit. They had like a committee. If you wanted some..."

"...body dead, you had to come to the committee and there was a vote."

"Like the Mob?" Prince interrupted.

"Not quite, but with the committee, when they voted and if there was a split decision they'd flip a coin, and just like that a life was saved or loss. Long story short, they ran them Choppa city niggas out of the city and they ended up in Fort Myers. So, Chuck the old head of their clique sent a hit on Ramirez, but the mission failed and Hitman's lil brother was killed. So, he been kinda low key hiding out ever since then. Everybody knows the committee was responsible for the hit. Hitman blames himself for his lil brother death. Rumor has it, that Choppa believes that you are the one responsible for robbing and shooting him."

"What, why would I wanna rob his broke ass? He gets his work from us," Prince asked confused.

"That's exactly what I was thinking, I really don't know but that's the reason for Hitman's presence. Of course, we know what's Baby's intentions."

*So, Hitman is Choppa's homie,*' Prince thought, now shit is starting to make sense. "Thanks Omar man, I have to make a run and update the gang on this shit, imma let you know when we get some shit together," Prince stated pulling out.

Prince pulled off the block and hopped on the express way headed to the Low when a sheriff squad car pulled behind him. He checked his speed. *'I not speeding,'* he thought. "Be cool, be cool," he told himself thinking about the gun that he had under his seat. About a quarter mile later he was pulled over.

"License and insurance sir," the tall bald sheriff asked.

Prince gave him his ID. "I don't have my license yet, but here's my information."

"Can you cut the car off please, sir?" the sheriff asked politely. Prince complied. Another squad car pulled up and two officers stepped out. Five minutes later four more squad cars pulled up.

*'What the fuck?'* Prince thought.

"Hands where I can see them," a young white officer demanded.

"Step out of the car," another one screamed. Prince put his hands up and slowly exited the car. He was roughly thrown to the ground and taken into custody. The medal door of the interrogation room jerked open snapping Prince out of his thoughts. Then in walked Detective Hollywood and Detective Sarson, they entered the room with a bag of Popeye's chicken and a large coke. Prince sat up straight.

"What time is it and why do y'all have me here?" He asked. Detective Johnson handed Prince the bag of food, he wanted to turn it down but his stomach wouldn't let him.

"We'll tell you everything, but first I want you to eat up so you can get your mind right," Hollywood offered.

*Fuck it,*' Prince thought smashing his food. Both Detectives left and came back after he was done eating.

"Okay, now it's time to get down to business," Detective Hollywood stated pulling out a folder from his brief case. "You've been a very busy man Prince," Detective Hollywood spat.

"And at such a young age too," Detective Sarson added. Detective Hollywood dropped an array of pictures on the table and then scattered them around. Prince kept his poker face but on the inside his stomach was doing flip-flops.

"Do you recognize any of these men in these pictures?" Detective Hollywood asked.

"Nope," Prince stated.

"Well, I beg to differ," Detective Sarson stated. Prince looked at her stone faced. "We know for a fact that you killed these ten men and justice will be served, we have an eye witness that can place you at the murder scene," she smirked.

"Do you recognize the person in this picture?" Detective Hollywood asked. Prince looked at the picture but didn't say anything. "Of course, you do," he added, "rumors have it, that this young man, Zaytige Hamilton, aka Lil Zay was like a little brother to you."

"Word is you had a real soft spot for the lil guy," Detective Sarson butted in.

"So, once he was killed you led a team of killas and killed all of these guys in revenge of Lil Zay's death," Detective Hollywood smiled.

"Now, we know you didn't act alone, and since you don't have a record and seem like a nice young man, we decided to give you an opportunity to help yourself," Detective Sarson added.

"Now, get to talking," Detective Hollywood demanded.

'These muthafuckas haven't even read me my rights,' Prince thought. "Y'all done?" Prince spoke. "For the record," he continued, "I don't know shit about no murders and I haven't killed no-fucking-body and any further questions y'all could take it up with my Lawyer. Now, can I get that phone call please?" Prince stated cockily.

"Listen hear you piece of shit," Hollywood snapped grabbing Prince by his collar. "We tried to help you, you little low life, black monkey muthafucka, but now your ass is grass, see we have a witness that can place you at the murder scene and that's willing to testify against you, you're done!" Prince yanked away. Detective Sarson grabbed her partner's arm slightly offended by his racial slurs.

"Let's go, he's not worth it." Detective Hollywood hesitantly let go of Prince's collar.

"Good luck in the big house ass hole."

"Thanks, for the food," Prince smiled.

"No problem, I spit in it," Detective Hollywood stated storming out with a smile of his own, "fucking nigger."

\* \* \*

Stevo stood in the mirror in the bathroom, he'd just took a shower and got dress. He was taking the braids outta his dreads. He put on his Gucci bandana letting his dreads hang over it. He was fresh from head to toe. He topped his appearance off with a squirt of exclusive cologne.

"Yo Rick, you ready my nigga?" Stevo yelled into the bedroom where Rick Rick was getting dressed. They had switched out of the hotel they were in into an Airbnb.

"Yeah, gang, I'm ready," Rick replied walking out.

"I still can't believe we left our fucking phones in that rental boi, Tokyo gone go crazy," Stevo complained.

"You talking about Tokyo, nigga yo ass need to be worried about Jasmine, that thick bitch that be stalking yo ass," Rick joked.

"I know Valo'nem been trying to call us like a muthfucka," Stevo spat.

"I doubt it, they know we gangsters," Rick joked, "we can handle ourselves."

He actually was in a good mood. He'd had a nice long conversation with Brandi and he was feeling her. He realized she was a bad bitch and he loved the way she talked, and the way she handles herself. They were waiting on King Lando, he was on his way to pick them up. He wanted to talk to them about yesterday. It worked out because after last night, they rushed to the airport to exchange their rental and left their phones in the car, rushing away from the scene and shit. The rental place was so pack they'd yet to locate their phones.

They had no idea that Ondat, Valo, and Smooth was killed. Prince was in jail, not to mention over a million dollars and 12 bricks were missing. They were in for a rude awakening when they got back.

Stepping out of the Airbnb they both jumped in King Lando's Cadillac truck. Some dude that they didn't know was driving. King Lando and Delyuntay was sitting in the second row so Rick and Stevo jumped in the third row.

"What's up shawty?" King Lando asked shaking both guys hands.

"Shit gang, just another day," Stevo replied.

"That's what's up." They all made small talk until they arrived to the baby mansion.

"Welcome to my home," King Lando announced. They all got out the car, and Rick Rick had to admit to himself that he was slightly impressed, especially seeing all the Foreign cars in the drive way. Once inside, Delyuntay led them to a big living room equipped with a plush all white sectional sofa, an 80-inch television set with surround sounds. In front of the sectional was a long glass table with bowls of exotic weed inside, all flavors. They sat down and King Lando threw them both packs of backwoods. They all rolled up backwoods apiece. Blowing smoke in the air King Lando spoke.

"Say mane, I really appreciate that shit y'all did for my fam shawty, that shit was gangsta. I could never repay y'all."

"Man, it wasn't nothing, we were just in the right place at the right time," Stevo stated.

"Them muthafuckas caught us lacking, I left my shit in the club, them pussy ass niggas got my cousin," Delyuntay stated shaking his head.

"What was that shit about tho? Why them nigga was gunning for y'all like that?" Rick Rick asked.

"We've been beefing with this nigga Blac Vontay and Chase since we were kids," King Lando admitted.

"Hold on, you say Blac Vontay and Chase?" Rick Rick asked.

"Yeah, why? You know them niggas?" Delyuntay asked making a funny face.

"This a small world gang, seems like we got a common enemy," Rick stated.

"What you mean mane?" King asked.

Stevo told them the full story starting with Baby and Mula, then he went on to tell them about the situation with Choppa and the whole situation about the robbery, the kidnapping, the whole nine yards. Once he was done, King Lando's mouth was hanging open.

"Them fuck niggas gotta go, see, shit been going back and forward between us. Them niggas just skipped town once we got on they ass, they shooters still here tho, but now thanks to y'all, we got one of their main killas out the way. That changes shit drastically. With them gone, shit wide open out this bitch, they were the only competition," King stated.

"We going to take care of that situation as long as them niggas in Miami."

"So, y'all doing pretty good for y'all self?" Rick Rick asked.

"We doing good because we the only muthafuckas with work, but we got some bull shit quality," Delyuntay stated. "And we're getting robbed," he continued shooting daggers at his big brother.

"What's the numbers on them thangs, what you paying?" Stevo asked.

"Mane, we paying 29 a chicken."

Stevo whistled and shook his head, "that's not too bad tho," he lied doing numbers over in his head.

"Shit, for how many we getting that number supposed to be lower," Delyuntay stated.

They felt comfortable talking freely around the DIME-BOYZ, I mean they did just catch two bodies for them and saved their lives at the same time, they felt bonded.

"How many y'all getting?" Stevo asked, his hand itching

"Anywhere from 10-15 a week."

*'Damn,'* Stevo thought, *'I can give it to them for 25 a thang and make 50 to 60 thousand a week off these niggas and the dope we got is so pure they'll triple their money.'*

Stevo pitched his game plan down to King Lando and promised that they could give them purer dope for about 50 thousand cheaper a shipment. King Lando wanted to jump for joy but he kept his composer, he was a firm believer that he had to see it to believe it. They agreed that King Lando'nem would have to come get the cocaine from Miami and just like that an unbreakable bond was created.

\* \* \*

**M**eanwhile, Chase pulled up to the scheduled area Tiffany was waiting for him at. He double checked his GPS just to make sure he was in the right place. It was very dark and his instincts told him to get the fuck back in the car, but his ego wouldn't allow him to.

*'If she on some funny shit imma cook this bitch,'* he thought.

"You made it!" Tiffany spat stepping out of the dark.

*'Where the fuck this bitch come from?'* he thought looking around. "Damn shawty, you can't be sneaking up on a nigga like that mane," Chase stated with his heart beating out of his chest.

He noticed that she looked like she'd been crying so he asked. She looked at him and broke down in tears. He rushed over to console her. He wasn't used to seeing her this vulnerable and it actually hit a soft spot that he didn't know he had. They embraced for a minute, then finally letting go of each other.

"Here," he spoke handing her a small envelope containing 50 thousand. "You did good shawty, you really proved yourself, I fuck with you the long way."

She took the money and couldn't help but to think that she'd just sold her soul. Chase got a phone call, he recognized the number and answer instantly.

"Man, big bruh, I got some bad news," the caller stated.
Chase took a deep breath then spoke, "lay it on me."
"Man, them niggas got T-MAC, he gone bruh."
"Fuckkkkkk…." Chase screamed.

\* \* \*

Shootsum and Kill was tucked discretely in a stolen car not too far from where Chase and Tiffany talked. Flo felt that she was acting hella strange in the hospital, he felt she knew things that only a muthafucka that was actually there would have known. Something definitely wasn't right so he called his two lil killas to keep a tail on her.

"Yeah, dawg, that bitch is most definitely up to something," Kill stated.

"I agree," Shootsum stated.

"Look, he giving that bitch an envelope," Kill spat excitedly. "You getting this shit?" he continued.

"Yeah, dog," Shootsum replied recording everything on his iPhone.

They watched her hug Chase again and then looked around nervously. She then hopped in her car and sped off. Shootsum thought outside the box.

"Fuck that bitch, dawg follow dude ass. Let's see who the fuck he is……."

## Chapter (19)

*'I seen this nigga before,'* Flo thought as he was watching the video of Chase that Shootsum and Kill recorded earlier. He was wrecking his brain to try and place the name to the face in the video. His gut was telling him that Tiffany was acting off and he always followed his gut. All of a sudden, it hit him, "this snake ass bitch," he blurted. He held Shootsum's phone closer to his face as if he couldn't believe his eyes. He watched Tiffany and Chase embrace, he watched Chase hand her an envelope, he saw her crying in his arms and his nose flared. Flo slammed his fist together creating a loud smacking sound.

"I remember where I seen this nigga at," Flo spat angrily. Shootsum and Kill looked at Flo but didn't say anything. "This that nigga that was with Choppa at Rick Rick's birthday party, it was him, Choppa, and another nigga," Flo stated.

"He does fit the description of the nigga we chase that robbed Prince, what the fuck she doing with the opps?" Kill asked disgustedly.

"My point exactly," Flo spoke with gritted teeth.

"Look like this bitch going against the grain," Shootsum spoke stating the obvious.

"It's like he paying the bitch off or something, why else would he be giving her money in the middle of nowhere," Kill added.

"What the fuck, my brother hasn't been dead 24hrs and muthafuckas switching up." *'Yeah, why would he be giving Tiffany money?'* Flo thought. I gotta change my number ASAP. I have too many snakes in my grass, man I wish O-Dog was out, he would have been by my side right now. I can't get ahold of Stevo or Rick Rick, them fuck niggas don't have a clue, ole soft ass niggas; I can handle what's going on in these streets, fuck them pussy ass niggas.

Then Prince bitch ass ran off with the money and the work, imma kill that bitch ass nigga when I catch his snake ass. Damn, I have to come up with this money for Veronica. I can't beef with this bitch to, she made it clear that if she doesn't have her money we might as well kiss the kids. The heat is on now, niggas wanna disappear and hide like lil bitches. Seems like they abandon me too. Them fuck niggas gotta be going against the grain, with all this shit going on the least they could of did is call, them niggas not even checking in. I got something for all these fake muthafuckas. I'm on my cut throat shit. My blood brother dead, Dee Dee missing, Sasha in prison. I can't take this shit, I feel all alone out here mane. I'm thankful for my young killas from Milwaukee tho, they some stomp down niggas, with them I can take over Miami my damn self.

Flo was unaware of the fact that Rick Rick and Stevo lost their phone and that Prince was in jail.

"You okay big homie?" Kill asked snapping Flo out of his train of thoughts.

"Yeah, mane, I just got a lot on my mind, a lot of shit to process," Flo responded. For some strange reason, he had a strong urge to do a line of coke. "I want y'all to follow that hoe and snatch that bitch up when the times right."

"Sounds good my nigga, but what you want to do about that nigga we followed?" Shootsum asked referring to Chase. They'd really caught Chase slipping and followed him right back to his lil hideout.

"You already know mane, tonight....... we gone cook his muthafucking ass. We gone lay on em all night if we have to," Flo stated.

"Hopefully, we can catch all they ass together," Kill added.

\* \* \*

## - *Flo* -

Later on, that night me, Shootsum, and Kill was camped out at the address they that followed dude to, I later found out that his name was Chase. We were in a stolen Durango truck that Shootsum snatched up from downtown Miami. The lights to the house was on and we could see movement inside. I made out a shadow of about three people, I couldn't tell who they were, but I was determined to get them to come out that bitch.

"Why don't we just throw a rock through the window?" Kill suggested.

"You know what, that doesn't sound like a bad idea," Flo stated. They all had assault rifles. Everybody put on their mask. "Y'all ready?" Flo asked.

"Born ready dog, let's get this shit over with so I can bust y'all ass in some NBA 2k," Shootsum stated.

"You sound crazy as fuck, you know you not fucking in my business," Kill jokingly replied.

"We'll see nigga, let's handle this lil shit first, then I'm on yo ass," Shootsum joked.

I just looked at the lil niggas, I really admired how death didn't have no effect on them, how putting in work came natural to them. They were savage. It's like they didn't care if muthafuckas lived or died, and that shit turnt my savage up a couple notches. We all hopped out of the car with guns at the ready, Shootsum found a brick and through it threw the window, about 30 seconds later the front door opened and that's when all hell broke loose....

\* \* \*

Choppa, Hitman, Rocko, Blac Vontay, and Jason all lounged around the hideout. Chase and Baby had become so close that they were out handling some last-minute arrangements together, being sneaky of course. In fact, if Flo'nem would have pulled up 10 minutes earlier, they would have caught them leaving the house. Dee Dee was still tied up in the basement and was barely clinging on to her life. Rocko being the pussy hound he was had become obsessed with her. He was determined to get that pussy one way or another.

Feeling like he had enough and couldn't take it anymore, he got off of the sofa headed towards the basement.

Choppa looked at him, "you straight gangsta?"

"Yeah, I'm cool mane, I'm just about to go check on this lil hoe down stairs, we don't won't the bitch to die on us now do we?" Rocko replied. Choppa gave him a funny look then thought about it.

"Yeah, good idea dawg."

Rocko eased the door close that led to the basement and continued his way down to the bottom stairs. He felt his dick getting hard with anticipation. He peeked in the room that Dee

Dee was being held in, she was chained to the bed half sleep. She hadn't eaten in over 30 hours, she was losing weight and she was very weak. Looking at her in her panties and bra made Rocko's dick jump. Hearing the door open cause Dee Dee to jolt awake. She was trying to make out the figure that was coming toward her. It was dark, the light from the window illuminate through the crack of the window.

Rocko took off his shirt and threw it on the floor and put his gun on top of it. Seeing the bulge in his pants kinda woke her up more. Rocko crept up on Dee Dee and began rubbing on her body.

*'Please God don't let this nigga be on no rape man type shit,'* she thought, seeing the type of trance she had him in gave her an idea. Rocko rubbed her flat stomach and made his way to her boobs. Dee Dee just laid there, she thought about her uncle and all the times he'd sneak in her room and molest her. She thought about all the things she did to help get it over with quick. She thought about the last time he molested her and violated her in every hole, she thought about his last attempt, when she killed him.

She snapped back to reality. She knew she was too weak to fight Rocko off, she knew she had to use her head. Rocko found her to be so beautiful, so irresistible, he pushed her bra up and began sucking her titties softly. To Rocko's surprise, Dee Dee began to moan. That motivated him and stroked his ego. He began sucking on her neck, she moaned louder as if she was into it but if the room was brighter he'd seen the disgusted look on her face. Being the pussy hound, he was, he took off all of his clothes until he was complete naked.

He jumped on top of her and began kissing her face, he attempted to entered her super tight pussy. He roughly poked his dick at her entrance and mistaken her cries for moans of pleasure. A sharp pain shot through her pussy as he finally was able to enter her. He humped her like a mad man. Dee Dee just thought about her child hood when her momma used to keep her safe, she thought about all the happiest moments of her life, she thought about the **DIME-BOYZ**... *'man I wish my niggas was here,'* a tear fell from her eyes involuntarily. She hated her vagina, "you can have it, it useless," she remembered telling her uncle.

She felt herself being yanked and came out of her daze. Rocko tried to fuck her from behind but couldn't do it due to the fact that she was chained to the bed. Thinking with his dick, he stared at Dee Dee with lust and licked his lips, *'fuck it,'* he thought unchaining her.

*'Did this nigga just unchain me?'* Dee Dee thought with a newfound burst of energy.

Rocko continued to rape her. The pain didn't even affect her anymore, she just played along, she had a plan.

"Fuck yeah, take this dick shawty," he moans.

Dee Dee hated the fact that her pussy was becoming so wet, but she wanted it to because murder was on her mind.

"Damn, shawty, on my God this the best pussy ever," Rocko moaned, "you wet as fuck mane."

All the while Dee Dee was slowly moving toward his gun, his ego made him believe she was running from the dick. The thought of killing him made her pussy even wetter. As soon as she got her hands on his gun she began cumming on his dick.

"Oh, my God bitch, you cumming…" this was the best feeling Rocko ever had and he closed his eyes. "Damn, babyyyyy I'm cumming with you." He began busting the best nut in his life, the last but of his life. He collapses on the bed.

"Come on shawty, come ride this dick," he smiled not realizing Dee Dee had a smile of her own.

She slowly stood up, he still had his eyes closed. Once he opened them he almost shits himself because he was staring down the barrel of his on gun.

"Woah, woah, woah… wait, wait, wait…" he stutters.

"There isn't no wait muthafucka, you like rapping people, huh? Turn yo bitch ass around," Dee Dee screamed thinking about her uncle.

"Huh?" he asked confused.

"Don't make me repeat my fucking self," she stated like a mad woman. Rocko slowly turned around and Dee Dee smacked him in the back of the head with all her might with the gun. Knocking him simi unconscious.

She then got on top of him and began jamming the gun up his ass. He hollered.

"You bitch ass nigga, now you see how it feel to get fucked," she stated violently gun fucking him with his own gun. She thought he was crying, but once she really listened to him she noticed he was actually moaning. She thought she was tripping until he reached back to spread his ass cheeks. He began backing up on the gun moaning like a bitch.

"Awe hell nawl, you bitch ass nigga," Dee Dee yelled pulling the trigger shooting him multiple times up his ass killing him instantly.

\*   \*   \*

Meanwhile, Shootsum threw the brick through the window shattering it.

"What the fuck?" Choppa stated being caught off guard. Vontay reached for his gun while Jason went to the door to investigate, Hitman just sat there. Jason opened the door, he looked out but didn't see anyone.

"Must be one of y'all crazy ass hoes," Jason yelled back with a soft chuckle causing Choppa and Vontay to let they guard down, but not Hitman. With a sigh of relief, Flo, Shootsum, and Kill lurked behind the shadows watching Jason stalking him like pray. Kill looked at Shootsum shaking his head no, knowing how trigger happy Shootsum could be.

Once Jason completely stepped off the porch to examine the window, Flo nodded his head at an anxious Shootsum. Smiling like a kid in a candy store Shootsum came from behind the tree.

"Sup fool?"

Jason looked and when he saw Shootsum with that big ass AR-15 he didn't even reach for his gun and made a run for it.

*'Not today,'* Shootsum thought letting off the AR with determination. The bullets struck Jason as he was almost to the door causing his body to jerk violently. Flo and Kill came out of the shadows and began shooting the house up. It sounded like the fourth of July. Choppa and Vontay ducked for cover while Hitman began shooting back at them. Choppa started firing from behind the sofa blindly toward the window, Blac Vontay follow suite. Damn, Flo ducked a bullet barely missing him by an inch.

*'What the fuck?'* Dee Dee thought hearing all the gun fire upstairs. "I gotta get outta here," she whispered to herself. She looked around the basement and spotted a window, *'bingo,'* she thought. She walked to the window and to her surprise it was just a regular window. She found a chair and stood on top of it to open the window, she unlocked it and like magic it opened. She was about to climb out, but suddenly remembered she was naked. She went back to the room were a dead Rocko was laying and stepped over him, she shot the dead man in the face, "bitch ass nigga," she stated and began putting his clothes on. *'These fit skinny,'* she thought not believing her and Rocko wore the same size clothes.

She heard more gun fire upstairs, *'Goddamn, these muthafuckas got big guns,'* she thought checking Rocko's gun she took making sure she had ammunition. She went to the window and began to climb out, *'it's all or nothing,'* she thought jumping in survivor mode.

Choppa army climbed to the kitchen and cut on all the gas on the stove, "backdoor," he yelled to his cousin over the gun fire. Blac Vontay and Hitman crawled to the kitchen leading to the back door. He could smell the gas getting louder, "this house is about to blow, we need to get the fuck outta here," he yelled. "You hit," Choppa stated noticing the blood leaking from Vontay's leg.

"I know man, I know."

Choppa helped him out the back door and ran smack dead into Dee Dee. She had just made it out the window and was running toward the back, but seeing them she busted a u-turn and began running toward the gun fire. Choppa began shooting at her, she ran like her life depended on it. Everybody was still shooting at the house. Kill saw someone running out the gang way with no shoes on out the corner of his eye. He couldn't make out the figure, all he knew was that person had a gun. He aimed his gun at Dee Dee but before he can let off a shot she began open fire.

Kill ducked but caught a bullet to the arm causing him to drop his weapon. Dee Dee cut down the street running like a crack head. She became dizzy and she began running slower and slower, next, thing you know she collapsed. Seeing the dark figure drop Flo smelled blood and began advancing toward Dee Dee. Dee Dee was fresh outta bullets and just knew it was over, but she vowed she wasn't going to die begging for her life.

*'I'm a muthafucken DIME-GIRL, imma die like a solider,'* she thought. She heard the footsteps getting closer, she said a quick prayer then she opened her eyes because she wanted to look her killer in the eyes. She couldn't make out the figure that was standing over her. Shootsum stood over her with his gun trained on her face, but stopped dead in his tracks.

"It's a female he stuttered." He never kilt a female before and didn't think he wanted to

Flo unfazed by the gender pushed him aside, "I got this mane," but what he saw took his breath away. "Dee Dee?" he asked.

"Flo, Valo?" she asked confused. She asked not believing her eyes. He pushed out of the way guarding her with his life and kneeled down by DeeDee to pick her up.

"This my muthafucken sister, help me get her to the car," Flo ordered.

Dee Dee thought she was dreaming. "Is it really you?" she asked before passing out.

## Chapter (20)

"How she's doing doc?" Flo asked the neighborhood doctor.

"She'll be fine, she's dehydrated and weak, once these fluids enter her and she get some rest she's going to be as good as new," he replied starring at a sleeping Dee Dee.

*'Thank God,'* Flo thought. "What about my mans?" Flo stated referring to Kill.

"He's alright, the bullet hardly touched him, it skinned his arm, its nothing more than a flesh wound," the doctor stated.

"You lil pussy," Shootsum joked relieved.

Kill poked his chest out, "that's crazy, even bullets are afraid to touch me," he laughed.

Flo handed the doctor a wad of cash, "thanks for showing up at such short notice."

Doc pocket the money, he was an older while man in his mid-fifties, "anytime young man," he shook Flo's hand. "You just make sure she takes those pills on time and she'll make a full recovery," the doc paused, "it's kinda funny seeing you without your brother, tell him I said hello," doc said leaving out the door. Flo just stared at the back of his head, all of his emotions starting to rush back to his head.

"Don't trip baby bro, imma get all them niggas, even Stevo, Prince, and Rick Rick bitch ass for turning they back on us."

\* \* \*

Meanwhile, Stevo and Rick Rick flight landed at the Miami airport. They'd just left baggage claim and got the few bags that they did have and headed to the car.

"Damn, Joe, we about to be some rich ass niggas, wait until I tell Valo and Flo the type of numbers we gone be doing in Atlanta, shit about to get real," Stevo stated.

"On my momma," Rick Rick agreed while driving.

"Man, I'm just happy we were finally able to get our phones back," Stevo stated putting his phone on the charger.

"Hell yeah, I know Ondat and Prince'nem been catching all the plays," Stevo huffed.

"Hell yeah, I bet," Rick Rick agreed thinking about all the money he missed. Stevo phone came to life and instantly began going crazy with messages, Rick Rick's too; they both smiled.

"It seems like gang'nem missed us," Rick Rick joked without looking at his phone.

"Man, I hope they got some updates on Dee Dee for real because we got all the information we need to crush this Vontay nigga, real shit." Rick Rick looked over at Stevo and noticed he wasn't talking.

"Your cool gang?" Rick asked.

"Nawl, something isn't right boi." He looked at all his messages from Flo, he tried calling him.

*"The number you have reached has been disconnected please hang up and check the number as dialed error code106."*

'*The fuck,*' Stevo thought. He tried the number again and got the same result. "This some fuck shit," Stevo yelled. Unbeknownst to him, Flo changed his number. He tried calling Valo, but kept getting the voice mail. He tried Prince and kept getting the voice mail. He tried Ondat and got the voice mail also. He caught a funny feeling in his gut '*something isn't right*' he thought. He called Tokyo and she picked up on the first ring.

"Oh, my God, you okay baby? You had a bitch about to fly to Atlanta," she stated excitedly.

"Why the fuck you haven't been picking up your phone?" she asked mood changing all the sudden. "You been with a bitch? I've been worried sick about you!" she stated angry. He had her on the speaker phone.

"We lost our phones at the rental place and just got them back before we hopped on the plane."

"Are you okay?" she asked in a broken voice. He looked at the phone, "why wouldn't I be okay?" he responded.

Tokyo just stayed silent, "Bae, you got a number on Jade? I can't reach none of the guys," Stevo stated.

"Ummm, I think so, she probably doesn't won't to be bothered, she may still need some time."

Stevo laughed, "Valo got caught with his dick in the cookie jar again huh?" he asked.

"Wait, what?" Tokyo asked confused.

"What that nigga do this time?" Stevo asked.

"Baby haven't you watched the news?" she continued.

"The news? Why the fuck would I be watching the news when we run these fucking streets, we are the news," Stevo joked causing Rick Rick to smile.

Tokyo looked at her phone then it dawned on her, *they don't get Miami news in Atlanta,'* she thought. "Baby you don't know do you?" She asked as tears fall down her face.

"Know what girl?" Stevo asked sensing the seriousness in her voice. She was hesitant to tell him, she did not know how he'd react, she didn't want to be the one to tell him both of his best friends were dead.

"Baby nobody's heard from Flo or Prince and I'm sorry to be the one to tell you this but Valo and Ondat were gunned down they didn't make it." Stevo's heart dropped and Rick Rick side swiped a parked car.

"What bitch, don't fucking play with me like that, don't tell me no shit like that," Stevo snapped in disbelief.

"I'm so sorry baby, it's been a few days now and I thought you would have known by now."

Rick Rick pulled the car over, Stevo hopped out the car and threw up his guts. The tears wouldn't stop falling down his face. He hung up with Toke and tried the whole gangs' numbers again, but didn't get an answer.

"Fuck that shit, shoot to the hood this bitch gotta be wrong," Stevo snapped. They both hopped in the car and headed to the Low. They parked discreetly at the beginning of the block.

The block was dry as fuck. The hood was so hot you couldn't make a penny on the block. It was no secret that a war was going on among the hustlers and the police knew it too! Finding the top players involved in the massacre was priority to the MPD. That's all the men in blue wanted was justice, so they were making it hard to make money. You could barely walk on the block without getting stopped, they were truly out harassing every black man in the neighborhood.

Stevo scanned the block and was surprise at how junkies were walking around looking hopeless. A knock on the window cause both Stevo and Rick Rick to jump.

"Treal," Stevo stated.

"What's up big homie?" Treal answered.

"Hop in," Rick Rick stated. Stevo got out and let Treal hop in the front seat, he was a true gangsta and never let anyone ride in the back seat behind him. Rick Rick sped off.

"Man, were y'all been, shit been fucked up? I heard them niggas was looking for me," he stated hyped up.

"When bruh'nem funeral?" Treal asked without even taking a breath.

"Slow down lil homie, who looking for you?"

"Them niggas who kilt Valo, Smooth, and Ondat," he stated.

"Smooth dead too?" Rick Rick asked.

Treal looked at them like they were crazy, "what, y'all didn't know? They got my homies Chance and AJ to."

Stevo put his hands in his face and blew in them, "who did this shit?"

"Ion know, they came through the block and cornered bruh'nem in. I was in my room when they started shooting, I looked out the window and saw what was going on so I grabbed my shit and started shooting out the window. Them niggas was dressed up like plumbers and shit bruh, I dropped one of they ass tho," he stated referring to Rico. "Jason killed Valo to bruh," Treal stated.

"What, how you know that?" Stevo asked leaning up in his seat.

"I saw that shit with my own eyes, I was looking out the window. I would have smoked his ass but I ran outta ammo."

"I knew that bitch ass nigga was a snake!" Rick Rick stated stopping the car. "You sure lil nigga, because you better be sure before you say some shit that's gone get a nigga murked."

"Nigga, I seen that shit with my own eyes, on my gang, on Foe'Nem Grave," he stated referring to his Murder Gang clique. "Besides, that fool got smoked last night anyway," Treal stated with a smirk on his face.

Stevo look at him, "Yeah?" he asked, "by who?"

"Word on the streets is that Flo been putting his murder game down, him and three lil niggas," Treal stated referring to Lil

Discount as the third man. "They say he wacked Jason's uncle too!"

"Pimping?" Rick Rick asked.

"Yup, they say Flo been on a rampage!" Treal stated with admiration.

"How you know all this shit lil nigga?" Rick Rick asked.

"The streets big homie, I am the west side," Treal stated cockily, "but it's all over Facebook, R.I.P Jason and shit."

Stevo and Rick Rick was impressed at the fact that lil Treal dropped a nigga for the gang. To them that showed he had heart. They also liked the fact that he was knowledgeable. What impressed them the most was that he didn't ask them for shit in return and it seemed like the murder he committed didn't faze him and he was only 16.

"Say lil homie, run that shit down to me again and start from the top," Stevo stated relaxing passing him the blunt of exotic weed. Stevo phone rang and he picked it up.

"Bruh, where you at I need you."

"Kiesha? Stevo asked. "Yeah, it's me bruh, y'all back yet? I've been blowing y'all shit up, y'all good?"

"Hell nawl, somebody gotta die."

"Now we talking," Kiesha stated excitedly, "meet me at the address I'm about to text you, I gotta lotta shit to tell y'all."

* * *

**D**ee Dee sat upright on the comfortable bed she was laying in. She had an IV in her arm. She felt light headed and dizzy, *'Where am I?'* She thought. Her mouth was dry, she was dehydrated. Her body ached. She thought about the events that took place the night before. She thought about the rape, the shooting, the loud gun fire, and the escape. Flo saving her. She thought maybe she was dreaming, she tried to sit up and with a little effort she did. Kill walked in the room, he was all bandaged up but nothing major.

"She's woke," he yelled. She looked at him alarmed and sized him up, he did the same to her. *'Damn she bad,'* he thought to himself. She smirked, recognizing the looked.

"You shot me!" He stated handing her a cup of water. She looked at him but didn't say nothing or take the water. "It's not poising you know," Kill joked. Just as Dee Dee was about to say something slick in walked Flo.

"Flo," she yells with a ball of emotions. Flo rushed over to her and hugged her.

"Are you okay?" he asked her.

"Yeah, I'm okay,"

"I missed you sis."

"I missed you to bruh," she responded with a cracked baby voice.

"Baby and Mula ordered them niggas to snatch me," she stated emotionally.

"Here, drink this," he stated giving her the same cup that Kill gave her. She looked at the water and then looked at Kill. Flo noticed the exchange.

"Kill, this Deeahja; Deeahja, this is Kill."

"Nigga, don't be saying my government name I don't know this nigga," Dee Dee spat sassy.

"I remember her, she was at the party, right?" Kill asked.

"Yup, that's her the first lady," Flo stated. Kill smiled at the First Lady, she mugged him. Shootsum walked in and Flo introduced everyone.

"Where the real gang at?" Dee Dee asked shooting a shot at Shootsum and Kill. Flo gave her a sad look as he sat on the bed besides her.

"Look sis, what I'm about to tell you gone hurt your heart, but the revenge we seek is going to cleanse your soul."

He told her everything. He told her about Smooth, Ondat, and Valo getting killed. About Tiffany taking some sort of payment from Chase and how he felt she had some snake shit going on. He told her about Stevo and Rick Rick, and Prince turning their back on the gang and about his theory of them disappearing with all the money and drugs, leaving the gang for dead. He also told her how Veronica has been sending threats of what she gone do if she doesn't get her money. He left no stone unturned, by the time he was done they both had tears in their eyes and revenge on their heart's.

"Fuck them niggas, they were always on some Chicago shit anyway. Them bitch ass niggas, they bleed like we do."

"Yeah, they ass not welcome back out here, put the word out," Flo ordered. "If they ever come back I got 50 g's on their heads apiece."

"Damn, I'll love to collect on that," Shootsum stated. "Not if I catch them first," Kill countered.

"Don't trip, I haven't been spending my money. What I have plus, what you got, we should be able to pay the plug off," Dee Dee volunteered.

Flo blew out a sigh of relief, "that's something we need to look into asap because the streets been dry as fuck."

"Man, the streets on fire," Kill stated.

"We need to get rid of our enemies, eliminate anybody that isn't with us," Dee Dee stated. "We need to start our own shit, something we can build off of."

"Sounds good to me," Kill added.

"Since you're the only girl in the clique, we changed the name of the Low to D-Block," Flo stated.

Dee Dee smiled, "D-Block it is…"

\* \* \*

## - STEVO -

**M**e, Rick Rick, and Treal pulled up to the address that Kiesha sent us. It was a small house in a middle-class neighborhood, Kiesha greeted us at the door. She rushed into my arms and hugged me tight. I hugged her back. She let me go and hugged Rick Rick, and then she hugged Treal.

"Man, what's up with you shawty," Treal flirted.

Kiesha smiled, "Oh, right, lil ass boy, I see you've been busy," she stated referring to the body he caught. His name was buzzing.

"What's the word tho?" I asked.

Kiesha got emotional, "Stevo, I miss them already," she told me. "We have to get the funeral together, I hate this shit man. If shit wasn't bad as it is, the pigs done snatched Prince up," Kiesha stated.

"What for, and why haven't nobody bailed him out yet? Where is the lawyer?" I asked.

"They got him on like 4 or five bodies, he doesn't have no bail," Kiesha stated.

"Get the fuck outta here," I stated. "Where he at?" I asked.

"He's in the county, they saying they got an eye witness that can put him on the scene."

"Not for long," Rick Rick stated.

"Who they got?" I asked.

"Ion know, I couldn't get that information," she stated.

"What Omar say?" I asked.

"See, that's the thing, Omar ass been missing and the store been closed down and shit, but the Lawyer Desist Oceans is on it. She's trying to get him a bail."

"Fuck ma, this some bull shit. Have anyone of y'all heard from Flo… and what's up with Dee Dee?" I asked.

"Flo changed his number, I've tried calling his ass, but I didn't get an answer."

"Imma slide to his lil hide out and see what's up," Rick Rick stated.

"Yeah, do that, I have to go check up on Prince. Imma set a visit up and let y'all know, but in the meantime, y'all stay dangerous," Kiesha stated.

My phone rang and it was Tokyo so I answered.

"Baby, they chasing me and shooting at my car, oh, my God where are you I need you?" she screamed hysterically.

"Calm down baby, where you at?"

"I'm on belt line headed west."

"Okay, take that to the loop, get off and head toward the headquarters, imma meet you there be safe. Do you have yo gun on you?" I asked.

"Yeah, but I'm out of ammo baby, I've been busting back at they ass."

*'Damn my bitch gangsta,'* I thought. "Okay, stick to the plan, imma meet you there," I stated and hung up.

"You straight?" Treal asked.

"No, somebody shooting at my bitch we gotta go, you got some straps here ma?" I asked Kiesha.

"But of course," she stated grabbing a duffel bag full of guns. We all rushed out the door, all four of us headed to the headquarters....

## Chapter (21)

**W**e all hopped in the car with guns cocked and ready. I called Tokyo back and she picked up right away.

"Where you at ma?"

"I'm on the belt line and the car is still behind me, I can't see their faces because they got their fucking windshield tinted."

"What car are you in?" I asked her.

"I'm in your black Jaguar," she yelled.

I could tell she was talking to me through the car speakers but what caught my attention was the fact that she was in my Jaguar. Everybody that was somebody knew that Jaguar, they knew that was my car. I'm the only one in the city with the candy black on black XF sport with the black Forgies 22-inch rims. They had to be gunning for me, I just prayed that my shorty made it out safely.

"I have them by at least three cars bae," she yelled.

"We're almost there…" I heard gun shot rang out. **Boc, Boc, Boc, Boc.**

"Fuckkkkkk…" Tokyo yelled in frustration. My blood began boiling and I was ready to kill.

"You okay, ma?"

"Yeah, I'm cool, they shot out the back window tho, these muthafuckas trying to kill me bae."

"Where are you now?" I asked her in a panic voice.

"I'm getting off the belt line now about to pass KFC."

"Okay, take that main rode down three blocks and you're going to see the Audi," I stated.

We all jumped out the Audi on the block I told Tokyo to drive down. The way they were shooting I was afraid that we wouldn't make it to the headquarters so I decided to end this shit right now. Me and Kiesha stayed on one side of the street ducked off between two houses in the gang way. Rick Rick and Treal did the same on the opposite side of the street.

"What color car they in?" I asked her. "They in a silver Benz with black tints, it's two of them, same cars tho, I'm about to turn on main street now," she stated.

I see the Jaguar head lights zooming down the block. She had a nice lead on them and was able to make it pass us before the Benz hit the block. As soon as the Benz got close enough we all opened fire. We lit the muthafucka up. We had to let off about a hundred shots collectively when the Benz came to a halt. Kiesha must have reloaded because she was still shooting. I stood there with my mouth wide open.

*'What the fuck?'* I thought. The bullets were just bouncing off the Benz sort of like heavy rain would do.

Kiesha stop shooting, "that muthafucka bullet proof," she stated in disbelief. Another silver Benz pulled up behind it. I braced myself, I was out of bullets and I'm sure we were out gunned, but if I was to die I'll happily die with my gang. The second Benz back window rolled down slowly and a beautiful Cuban woman appeared. She looked me dead in the eyes.

"You must be Stevo," she asked licking her lips.

*'How this bitch knows my name?'* I thought, but I didn't respond. She extended a card out the window.

"Tell my cousins they have 24 hours to call me or things are gonna get very interested around here," she stated. She dropped the card out the window, I watch it land on the concrete, she smiled, blew me a kiss, and winked at me. Tokyo frowned and both cars sped off.

"What the fuck was that about?" Tokyo asked confused.

I picked up the card out the streets, it read 'Queena Fearis.' This Valo'nem last name. *'Tell my cousin they got 24 hours to call me,'* I repeat to myself.

"I think that was Valo'nem plug," I stated.

"Why the fuck would Valo'nem plug be shooting at us?" Rick Rick asked.

"I don't know, but we definitely gotta get to the bottom of this shit. It's gone be a little hard to shoot muthafuckas that got bullet proof cars and shit," I sated.

"Yo we gotta get outta here," Treal spoke up. We all hopped back in our cars heading to Tokyo's....

\* \* \*

"The headquarters got hit," Lil Discount spoke through the phone. He was on the phone with Flo hiding out in one of the spots on the block, "police every fucking where."

"Fuck you mean got hit?" Flo asked. He'd just done a line of powder and his blood was pumping.

"Man, a muthafucka came through spraying the whole fucking block up mane, they had to let off at least 2-3 hundred shots," Lil Discount stated.

"2-3 hundred shots?" Flo asked. "So y'all just let a muthafucka come through and wet up the block?" Flo screamed through the phone.

"Hell nawl, big homie, it wasn't nothing like that, now you know I let that Draco dump, but the bullets just bounced off that muthafucka."

"Fuck you mean just bounced off that muthafucka?" Flo asked.

"Mane, them muthafuckas was in some bullet proof Benz," Lil Discount stated.

*What the fuck? Bullet proof Benz? Yeah, we underestimated these niggas. They playing for keeps, shit really about to get real, nothings off limits,'* Flo thought to himself. He was thinking that the hit was Baby'nem. "Okay, just lay low mane, imma get with you," Flo stated.

He was in his Range Rover headed to meet his gun connect Shakee.

"One mo thang big homie, we outta work," Lil Discount stated."

*'Damn,'* Flo thought. "Sit tight and shut everything down and imma be with y'all when shit die down," he stated hanging up. He made it to Shakee condominium in record time.

"Shakee, my man," Flo greeted Shakee slapping hands with the guy.

"I'm surprise to see you," Shakee responded. "What's been up with you guys?" he asked. Shakee was a thin yellow kid that O-Dog met years ago.

He wasn't really Flo's friend, he was O-Dog's guy but they had been doing good business since O-Dog been in the slammer and the money had been rolling in. Shit was sweet on both ends.

"What's up man, you have that order I requested?" Flo asked.

"Yeah, of course," Shakee responded pointing to the three duffel bags. Flo walked over to the duffel bags and peeked inside them and smiled.

Inside the duffel bags was guns and ammunition. Flo threw a duffle bag at Shakee. He started to open the bag and count the money

"What, you don't trust me?" Flo asked nose flaring.

"No, it's nothing like that, it's just business bruh."

"It's just business? Nigga, if you don't trust me I don't trust you," Flo spat pulling out his gun.

"Woah, woah, woah, it's me baby, I trust you, I know that lil money don't mean nothing to you, I know it's all there." Shakee stated in a trembling voice.

"Nigga, it's obvious you don't trust me," Flo spat shooting Shakee four times in the face. Flo picked up the three duffle bags full of guns, then he picked up the duffel bag that he brought to Shakee. It was full of newspapers, he had no intentions on paying Shakee, he felt that if he didn't have enough money to pay his plug, he damn show wasn't going to pay the gun connect. He looked at Shakee's dead body. "You should have trusted me nigga," he stated seriously.

He knew O-Dog was gone be mad, but shit'd, *'it is what it is,'* he thought. Flo searched the whole house and found two more bags of guns and another bag of ammunition. He also found a hundred and twenty thousand dollars cash. The whole time he was searching the house Shakee's phone kept going off. Flo phone rang he picked up right away, "Hello?"

"Guess who I got the drop on?" Shootsum asked.

"Who?" Flo asked anxious.

"Rick Rick," he stated.

"Where at?"

"On D-Block."

For the first time since he was a child Flo second guessed himself. He thought about all the shit him, Rick Rick, and Stevo went through. He almost called it off then he thought about Valo and how them niggas just up and abandoned them (so he thought).

"It's a go," he told Shootsum. "Kill him."

He wiped down everything he touched and left the same way he can in.

Rick Rick left Tokyo's Salon. He went looking for Flo to warn him about his plug, to let him know that they were gunning for him. He arrived on the block by himself, Treal decided to stay with Stevo, not to mention all the bad bitches that was buying hair and getting their nails done. It was safe to say Treal was excited. The block was dry, there wasn't a lot of fiends out but there were some. Rick Rick saw Lea and Rideout and got out the car.

"Yo Lea," he yelled. Lea, who was looking for a fix saw Rick Rick and almost broke her neck to get over to him.

Unlike everybody else, Rick Rick and Stevo still had work. Stevo always brought his dope upfront, he was still sitting on over three bricks. Three bricks in the drought was like six bricks. Rick Rick had about a brick and a half in ounces because he played the block plus, he knew where Prince dope was hidden. He vowed to keep Prince shit going so that when he got out he'll have a big bag waiting on him.

"Boy am I happy to see you. Look Rick, I don't know if you know but word on the street is that you got fifty thousand dollars on yo head."

*'Fifty thousand dollars,'* Rideout thought, *'I could use that.'*

"Yeah?" Rick asked un-bothered not knowing Flo was the one who put the bounty on his head. He actually thought she was lying on some crack head scamming shit. "These pussies don't have the balls to play with me."

*'I ain't no pussy,'* Rideout thought, *'I ain't these young niggas, imma take your dope and smoke that shit up, and collect that fifty thousand dollars, how bout that!'* Rideout thought easing his knife out his back pocket. He was high out his mind, he actually did meth too.

"You know I had just warned Valo about some snake shit right before he died. Just watch yo back, that's all I'm saying.

*'She actually looks sincere,'* Rick Rick thought. He reached in his pocket and gave her a fifty, she thanked him and bought a hundred piece. She tried to hurry off to get high but Rick grabbed her arm.

"You saw Flo?" Rick asked.

"I seem him two days ago, he's been a lil off, he been shooting shit up and doing all type of crazy shit since his brother been gone. I'm not fucking with him like that right now."

"Where did you see him at?"

"He was with Lil Discount and the other two boys he be with all the time, the ones who always got new cars and shit," she stated referring to stolen cars.

*'Shootsum and Kill,'* Rick thought.

"There they go right there," Lea pointed. Rick looked up and to his surprise it was Shootsum and Kill heading his way.

What caught his eyes the most was the fact that Shootsum had a mug on his face with a gun in his hand. Rick Rick street instincts kicked in, he didn't know what his problems was but he wasn't taking no chances, he discretely pulled out his gun. *'Maybe she wasn't lying about that bounty,'* he thought.

Rideout, catching him off guard extended the knife with a full swing slicing Rick Rick down the ear and neck. Rick grabbed his neck in surprise, Rideout went for his gun, he had that crack head strength. Rick was trying to hold his neck with one hand and at the same time keep a hold of the gun. Lea leaped up and jumped on Rideout's back clawing at his eyes. That gave Rick Rick enough time to recover. Rideout slung Lea to the ground and advanced on Rick Rick.

Rick looked up just in time as Rideout was rushing toward him with the knife. Rick Rick raised his gun and shot him twice in the chest then he stood over him and shot him in the face.

"Fuck you think this is?" Rick asked the dead man.

A shot rang out, followed by multiple shots. He ducked and looked up as Shootsum was about to take aim again until Kill screamed, "there go 12 folks." Seeing them freeze up gave Rick Rick all the time he needed.

"What? Fuck the police these niggas trying to collect on this bounty huh, imma show they ass I'm a gangsta." Rick took aim, **boom, boom, boom, boom,** his first shot struck Kill in the shoulder. Yup, the same shoulder Dee Dee shot him in.

"Fuck!" Kill yelled. The police made it to the block but Shootsum began shooting at the police car striking the officer in the neck, he crashed into the street light.

Rick Rick let off about 15 more shots. Shootsum let off about 20 shots as Rick Rick took off down the block. Kill sent some shits his way but he managed to dodge them all. Shootsum started to chase him but decided to help Kill into the car instead. He knew by him shooting a police officer shit was about to hit the fan and he didn't want to stick around for it. Police siren were heard in the distance as Rick Rick manage to make it back to the car and sped off.

*   *   *

Tiffany sat on the small chair cramped up with her legs folded. She was sitting in the hospital were Jade was recovering. She was reading a book called 'Drug Lords' by her favorite author Ghost. She barley ever left. She stayed by her side every day since she discovered that it wasn't Valo in the room dead but someone who looked like him. They eventually found the room that he was in but when she saw his body he didn't look nothing like his self. The bullets blew his face up and added about fifteen more pounds on him, she was devastated.

"What did they do to you my baby?" she cried when she verified the body. Flo was in no condition to do it, he wasn't in the right state of mind so he asked Jade to do it for him.

He didn't want to see his brother like that. Tiffany still couldn't believe it. *'Valo is actually dead,'* she thought rubbing her stomach. She had a lot on her mind, Valo and Smooth funeral was only two days away. Ondat family held a private gathering with only family members allowed. His family had him cremated. She was happy that the funeral director convinced Flo that having a close casket was the best way to be remembered. He convinced him that celebrating life at a funeral was way more appropriate then celebrating death. Flo agreed, he honestly didn't want to see his brother in a casket at all, neither did she.

She wanted to remember him like he was, full of life and happy. She didn't know how she was gone make it through it all, but she knew she had to be strong. Dr. Ruby Griffin was assigned to watch over Jade. She just wanted to monitor her status and keep a close eye on her. She walked in with a big bright smile on her face. She was in a beautiful mood, she was on cloud nine. Thanks to Chase, who has been fucking her like a porn star every night, not to mention this morning. That's why she was in such a good mood.

He needed somewhere to lay low and she needed someone to stay with her. She felt so lonely being home all alone, she also missed coming home to a warm body and some good sex. She actually felt Chase was an upgrade. She knew nothing about his life of crime. She had her suspicion tho, but the dick made her over look all the red flags, so he milked the situation and so did she. Not to mention, he loved her pussy. It was the perfect situation and the perfect hideout. The perfect opportunity. He was actually attracted to her tho.

"How are you feeling today?" she asked a sleeping Jade as if she could hear her. She checked her heart rate and blood pressure. Tiffany put the book down and began watching her intensely.

"Is everything okay with her doc?" Tiffany asked.

"Yes, she's actually doing good, she just tired you know."

"Wow, that's incredible. Do you think she's going to be messed up?"

"Not at all child, but somebody killed her man for God sakes, she's just in shock but she'll be okay. She has a lot to live for," the doc winked pointing at her stomach.

*'Oh, God please no,'* Tiffany thought. "Please, tell me that doesn't mean what I think it mean doc?" Tiffany asked frowning.

"Yes, congratulations! You're going to be an aunt, she's about a month along, that's why she's sleeping so much. I ordered her to stay here so we can run some test. Don't worry though she's fine, she just needed some rest."

Tiffany felt herself getting sick, and then she felt dizzy, she rushed to the bathroom that was connected to the room and threw up her guts. This can't be happening, how the fuck are we both a month along, and pregnant by the same person? She's my fucking sister, blood sister... oh, my God, our kids are gonna be brothers and cousins.

"Are you alright?" Dr. Griffin asked.

"I'm fine, just something I ate," she lied. Tiffany splashed her face and dried it off with a towel. I gotta get outta here. She emerged out of the bath room. "I'm going home to change my clothes and shower. Call me when she wakes up, I'll be back."

"Okay, child, I will. Are you sure you're okay?"

"Yeah, I'm fine, this hospital food doesn't agree with my stomach."

"Go get some rest and I'll call you when she wakes," Dr. Ruby smiled.

*'Okay will do,'* she thought leaving out. "Fuck, fuck, fuck… I can't let her have that baby. I have to convince her to get an abortion…"

## Chapter (22)

**W**ord spread like wild fire about the attempt on Rick Rick's life. He was mad, he was on edge, he was paranoid, but above all he was confused.

'Why in the fuck would my own homie put fifty gees on my head? They say the best way to kill a snake is to cut off his head. I got to test that theory,' Rick thought. And, he tried, every chance he got he was out looking for Flo and his Clique. Rick Rick, Stevo, Treal, Kiesha and Biggs shot up every known spot Shootsum and Kill was known to hang out at. Lil Discount caught Stevo coming out the mall and opened fire on him in board daylight, almost taking his life. Stevo vowed to kill him next chance he got.

"I almost had that nigga big homie."

"Who?" Flo asked.

"That nigga Stevo," Lil Discount yelled pumped up. "That fuck nigga fast tho, his bitch ass ran back in the mall. I was this close," he stated with his thumb and index finger.

"Don't trip tho, we gone get them fuck niggas."

"On foe'nem grave," Lil Discount stated.

\*     \*     \*

**R**ick Rick, Stevo, Treal, Kiesha, and Biggs had successfully taken over the Headquarters. Moving out anyone that wasn't with the movement. Omar was supposedly sick out of town with the Corona virus. Kiesha proved to be deadlier then anyone would ever imagine, but so was Dee Dee, she'd already killed two of Stevo soldiers. She was by herself coming from the mall and spotted them talking to some women. She simply threw on one of her hoodies that was in the truck parked and crept up on them, they never saw it coming.

Flo, Lil Discount, Shootsum, Kill, and Dee Dee took over the Low and renamed it D-Block, after Dee Dee. The streets were buzzing about the war, niggas were starting to choose sides, and shit was heating up. The streets were hot as a fire cracker after Shootsum shot that police officer in the neck. It was a hundred-thousand-dollar reward for any information leading to the arrest of the suspects. The streets weren't talking tho, everybody was shaken. Lea was picked up for arm robbery and was in the process of taking a 2year deal.

Overall tho, everybody was waiting on the funeral which was one day away. O-Dog had called countless times trying to squash the beef.

"Bruh, I respect you and I love you, you my brudda, but it's up there and it's stuck there. That nigga tried to kill me. These fuck niggas got the nerves to bury that rat ass nigga Smooth next to a gangsta like Valo, hell naw gang, I can't go for that shit," Stevo snapped.

"Bruh, we bruddas, y'all are literary beefing over some petty shit," O-Dog stated.

"Naw nigga, we bruddas, me, you, Rick and Prince, them niggas was our friends, you always known them fuck niggas was jealous of us. We turnt they savage up. We turnt them niggas into killas. That nigga Flo just up the ante to a hundred thousand dollars on all our heads out here, you call that loyalty? Fuck that nigga, he's a bitch," Stevo snapped.

"Look gang, I love both of y'all and I hate that y'all beefing, imma pray for you niggas but I gotta go we about to do count. Ondat said get at him tho, he says he need some answers because he really fucked up about his brudda," O-Dog stated. He was on his burner iPhone in his jail cell.

"Imma get with him, I got the lawyer on him and Prince's cases, but it's not looking good for Prince. We can't find that hype bitch that told on him. They hiding that bitch. Without her they don't have a case," Stevo stated.

"Y'all niggas wild for letting her walk away, she was supposed to been six feet," O-Dog scoffed.

"I know gang, but them niggas kilt Lil Zay and we was on red mode. We caught about ten of they ass that day, blew up the crib and all type of shit."

"I know, everybody knows about the 10 murders in two hours, you niggas wild," O-Dog stated.

"Before you hang up imma keep it real with you gang, we're going to that funeral, Valo was our brudda and we have to pay our respects. Fuck that bull shit Flo on, Valo died like a gangsta and I miss my nigga."

"I understand that, but please don't act a fool at foe'nem funeral."

"Naw, we not on that type of time gang, we're just going to show our respect. Can't say what's gone happen if they pop off tho," Stevo stated.

"Keep me posted, I gotta go, love gang."

"Love," Stevo replied hanging up. *'Them nigga gotta know we coming to that funeral, how can we not,'* Stevo thought...

\* \* \*

Flo walked into the dealership, it was him, Lil Discount, and Dee Dee. He was on the phone patching things up with Veronica. She was deeply saddened by Valo's death.

"I'll see you at the funeral," Veronica stated.

"So, are you going to call your dogs off?"

"Sure, for now. I hope you are not going to have a problem getting my money with your senseless street troubles."

"Don't worry, it's under control, I just need more time," Flo pleaded.

"Two weeks after the funeral should be enough time?"

"Yes, I can make that happen."

"But of course, you will, the shipment would be there tomorrow," she stated hanging up.

"Bitch," Flo stated stuffing the phone in his pocket. *'This bitch knows the funeral tomorrow,'* Flo thought. "Loso my man," Flo greeted the dealer.

"Flo, what's up?" Loso asked shaking Flo's hand. He was also on the phone with his freaky black stallion, as he would call her. He wouldn't look him in the eyes.

"Let me have a word with you," Flo demanded.

"Sure, right this way," Loso stated leading the hoodlums to his office. Lil discount was the last one inside and he locked the door behind him, Loso got nervous.

"What's up Flo?" Loso asked nervously.

"Clam down, have a seat." Loso sat.

"There is a slight change of plans, tomorrow I will be picking the shipment up myself from here."

"You're kidding right? There's no way I could do that, Veronica don't won't any drugs in this place, and she's adamant about keeping this place clean. What's wrong with you guys swapping cars with the compartments, that's been working brilliant?" he asked almost pleading at the same time.

"Are you done?" Loso just looked at Flo. "It's none negotiable. My brother funeral is tomorrow and with everything that's going on its best we just do it this way. Understood?" Flo spat.

"I don't know Flo man, Veronica a kill me." Lil Discount cocked his gun causing Loso to jump.

"Okay, it's understood."

"Good," Flo stated.

"One more thing…" Dee Dee stated as they were leaving out. "One word to Veronica about this and I'll cut your dick off and shove it in your mouth."

Biggs sat in the small apartment that Valo and Flo use to live in. He was sitting at the table with Stevo discussing business amongst other things.

"We don't have any work left bruh, it's ugly out there in those streets," Biggs complained.

"I know, I'm working on it," Stevo responded, "I'm waiting on Fat Sosa to get back at me about that situation as we speak."

"Look bruh, you need to let me put that play down, I really been doing my homework and tomorrow is the day," Biggs pleaded.

"Ion know, it's a little risky my boy," Stevo countered.

"Not at all, see this the lick, I got my bitch Stacy on Loso heels. She been fucking him really good for about two weeks now. She got the nigga whipped, she says he with all that kinky shit. Long story short, he promised her a shopping spree tomorrow but called and backed out. He says he can't leave the shop because he got some business to handle. She offered to come to the shop, and when she went to the restroom that's when Flo and his clique came through. She says she overheard him saying that they are coming to pick up the product from the shop after the funeral."

"Are you sure that's what she heard?" Stevo asked.

"I'm positive," Biggs responded.

"So, that mean we hit the dealership before the funeral over," Stevo stated with a smile.

"Now you're following me my nigga," Biggs smiled...

* * *

**B**aby, Mula, Chase, Choppa, Hitman, and Blac Vontay all sat at the round table at Dr. Griffen's house. She wasn't home so Chase invited them over.

"So, these niggas having a funeral tomorrow huh? I say we light that bitch up," Hitman stated.

"We gone do better than that," Mula stated. "We're going to light that bitch up and burn it to the ground," Mula smiled.

"The whole city coming out, now I'm not the smartest man in the world, but if a nigga die that was making me all that damn money I'm sure as hell will be at his funeral," Baby stated.

"So, who are you speaking of?" Chase asked.

"Them niggas plug," Baby stated clapping his hands together.

"How happy you think the plug gone be if we shoot up the funeral while he in there?" Choppa asked.

"You right, that's the reason we just gone lay on the shit. We'll be able to spot the plug, he either gone be extremely low key or extremely loud. He shouldn't be that hard to spot. But," Baby continued. "If that muthafucka don't show up we light that muthafucka up, but if he does show up we wait until he leaves and follow him. As soon as he leaves we light that bitch up and wipe they ass out."

"Assuming it's a he," Hitman spoke.

"What you mean assuming it's a he? Of course, it's a he," Chase stated.

"Nigga everybody thought it was a he when Sasha was flooding the streets, but in fact it was a she," Hitman stated.

"Yeah, he not lying, have muthafuckas killing all the wrong muthafuckas, but he or she, which ever one it is be on point because they might just be prepared for us. They gotta know you coming to that funeral, how can they not?" Baby stated......

\* \* \*

The big day had finally arrived, the day that Valo would be laid to rest. Everybody that was somebody couldn't wait to attend the funeral. It was expected to be over 300 people in attendance. Flo paced back in forward in his condominium. He was freshly dressed in a black tuxedo and he still couldn't believe his brother was dead. He tried to think about all the good old days, but kept quickly dismissing them because they included the DIME-BOYZ. He hated them, he hated their guts.

He wanted nothing more than to see them in a casket alongside Baby in his clique. Dee Dee knocked on the door breaking his train of thoughts.

"The limo here bruh."

"I'll be right out," he replied. He went to the mirror and wiped his eyes. He hadn't even realized he'd been crying. He quickly went to the sink and splashed some water on his face. "Get it together Flo," he told himself.

The ride to the funeral was a long one. There were no words exchanged. Revenge was heavy on everyone's' heart. The Pastor, Pastor Jenkins was from the streets, he'd did a total 360 but was always in the know. So, in agreeing to do the funeral he had strict rules. There would be no guns allowed inside the church. Everyone would be searched at the door. Flo felt the limousine come to a halt. He looked out the window and realized that they'd arrived. He swallowed a perk 30 washing it down with a bottle water. They exited the limo and went into the church.

*'Damn this bitch crowded,'* he thought. They were respectfully searched. No exception! Shootsum and Kill wasn't feeling the no gun rule, but they obligated for the sake of the funeral. Flo and his clique were seated in the front row, the first person he noticed was Omar. He stood up and they embraced, DeeDee followed suite. He had a lot of questions for Omar but respected the fact that, despite whatever he had going on, he made it to the funeral. The funeral was like a fashion show. Everyone wore they best clothes.

Women that didn't even know Valo claim to know him for the sole purpose of getting close to the ballers, shit was crazy. The funeral was a close casket event, so there was a big picture of Ja'Valo sitting next to the casket. It was from Rick Rick's party.

*'I love that picture,'* DeeDee thought. There was another picture of Valo, Flo, and Sasha in the Wisconsin Dells when they were about 12. Flo felt a hand on his shoulder and jumped, he went for his waste but it was empty. He looked up only to see a smiling Veronica accompanied by Queena.

"How are you holding up?" she asked as they embraced.

"I could be better, I could be worse," Flo stated. He hugged Queena.

"Hi cousin," she stated. They actually stood out. They were both drop dead gorgeous with broken English, not to mention the six henchmen they arrived with that was outside waiting in two dark SUVs. The pastor began to speak.

"We are gathered here today to celebrate the life of the late Valo. See, this young man right here…" he stated tapping the casket, "he was living. See, some guys be living and some guys be living if you follow what I'm saying…"

He went on about what a great young man Valo was and how he died young and that's when the double doors to the church swung opened. Everyone stopped talking, you could literary hear a pen drop. Flo stood up, so did Omar and Veronica.

"Is it really you?" Flo whispered to himself. Walking through the double doors with shackles on her feet, dressed in an expensive black lady tuxedo with her usual confident cocky sexy seductive walk was no other than Sasha….

## Chapter (23)

"**G**od damn, what are you doing to me baby? Fuck please don't stop," Loso moaned. Stacy had him with one of his legs on the desk as she was eating his dick. He grabbed the back of her head and began fucking her face. She took it like a champ, she began choking on his dick. Only because she knew it stroked his ego, she didn't even have a gag reflex. She pulled her head back and smacked him on the hand, she looked in his lust filled eyes.

"Did I tell you to touch my hair?" she scolded. She stood up, she was in her six-inch heels and some sexy black boy shorts with the matching bra set.

She grabbed the pink hand cuffs she brought along with her out of her purse. She'd been waiting on the right opportunity to use them. Loso eyes got big with lust, she knew he was with all the freaky shit so getting him in the cuffs would be easy.

"And what are you going to do with those my black stallion?"

She didn't respond, she just began cuffing his wrist onto the chair. Once she made sure he was tight and secure, she used the other pair of cuffs and cuffed one of his legs to the chair. Loso's dick was throbbing in anticipation, he loved the freaky shit she did to him. Stacy was actually enjoying herself, she was the freak of all freaks. She took pride in her task especially, when it came to sex. She placed Loso's free leg back on top of his desk and began sucking his dick again.

Once it became sloppy wet, she began sucking his balls while she was jagging his dick. She went lower and began licking his asshole. He began going crazy. She began jagging it faster while licking his asshole, she felt his dick began to swell and she knew he was close. She stopped licking his asshole and began deep throating him. She stuck a finger in his ass and he began cumming hard in spurts moaning like a bitch. She got up leaving to clean herself off.

"Where are you going?" Loso asked slightly alarmed in the compromising position.

"I'm going to clean up, I'll be right back we're not done yet big boy," she smiled seductively. She proceeded to walk away.

She went to the rest room and quickly cleaned up and got dressed. She then went around to the back door and unlocked it letting Biggs and Treal in. She walked up to Biggs and gave him a sloppy kiss. That gangsta shit turned her on. He knew what she had just got done doing because him and Treal was looking through the window. That was part of the reason Young Treal was looking at Biggs like he was about to throw up his guts.

'Did you just see this bitch eating ass nigga?' Young Treal thought. Loso heard a sound assuming it was Stacy and he began to feel his self-become hard again.

'I wonder what she got up her sleeves now?' Loso thought, 'I've never had my ass licked before that shit felt good.' He felt a presence and looked up and his heart dropped, and his dick deflated.

"What the fuck is this?" he asked. Biggs and Treal both had on a mask.

Biggs began pistol whipping him and knocking his front teeth out. He flipped the chair over and began kicking him in the ribs. Loso began coughing up blood. Biggs snapped back to reality, Treal was just starring at him in shock. Biggs squatted face level with Loso.

"I'm only gone asks you this once, where is the coke?" Loso looked at the closest that was located in his office and whisper something. Treal took that as a hint to him that something about the closest. Treal walked up to the closest and opened it.

Inside the closest, was a big long box sitting on a dolly. Young Treal ripped through the box, 'bingo he,' thought.

"Here it go," Treal yelled. Biggs threw him the duffel bag and Treal began quickly loading it.

Biggs looked back at Loso and noticed the safe under the desk, Loso was terrified. "What's the code nigga?" With a little extra effort Loso spat out the code. Biggs opened the safe and took all the money out of it becoming a hundred thousand dollars richer. Once they were done they grabbed the tape from the camera that had recorded everything.

"What we do about him?" Treal asked Biggs.

"You decide." He told him walking out, he wanted to see did the youngsta really have heart. Treal didn't even have to think as he pointed his gun at Loso and shot him three times in the chest. Biggs heard the gun shots and smiled.

*'That's settled then,'* Treal thought as they were leaving. Biggs sent Stevo a text that read, "Done!"

\* \* \*

Hitman, Baby, Mula, Choppa, Blac Vontay, and Chase were dressed in all black with Teflon bullet proof vests on. They were camped out in the daycare that they'd broke in. It was the only spot they could hide out and see all the action that was going on inside the church. It was kiddy cornered across the street from the church. They had their eyes on everything moving. Especially, when Veronica pulled up.

"That's the plug right there mane," Chase whispered excitedly.

"Can't be too sure, just because she Mexican or sum shit," Baby stated. Then the other SUV pulled up and Queena hopped out followed by all six henchmen.

"Nigga, now tell me that's not the plug?" Chase asked.

"He might be on to something," Mula stated.

"So, we wait to they leave, follow the plug and light that bitch up?" Choppa asked going over the plan.

"Yup, sounds about right," Hitman answered.

"Wait, what the fuck?" Baby stated. "Is that the U.S Marshalls?" Baby asked seeing the familiar van.

Blac Vontay looked squinting his eyes, "sho in the fuck is," he stated. They watched in silence as the U.S Marshalls escorted Sasha outside of the truck and inside the church.

"Nigga, that's Sasha!" Mula stated.

"How in the fuck..." Baby asked stopping in mid-sentence.

"You know when you locked up and a family member die they let you come to the funeral and shit," Blac Vontay spoke thinking about his dad. He'd heard the story about Sasha and secretly wished he could have eaten with her. They watched her go in the church.

"We still shooting this muthafucka up right?" Chase asked simi afraid to shoot while the Marshalls were inside.

"Nawl, we gone wait this one out, I'm not shooting while the fucking feds in that bitch, but as soon as they leave we lighting this bitch up," Baby stated....

\* \* \*

**A**ll eyes were on Sasha when she entered the double doors. Flo, who couldn't believe his eyes stood up. He watched Sasha walk, even with the shackles on her she had this seductively walk about herself. Mostly, everyone in the church recognized her and they all stood to their feet. She made it to the front row. She was literary a living legend and she looked great. She looked like she hadn't aged a bit. Flo walked slowly toward her still not believing his eyes. The Marshalls looked at him like they were about to protest, but the look Sasha gave them quickly changed their mind.

"Momma?" Flo spoke hugging Sasha tightly. She hugged him as best as she could. "I'm sorry momma, I was supposed to be there for him, I was supposed to protect him" Flo started but was cut off.

"It's okay baby," she stated consoling him. Flo felt a tear escaping his eyes. Sasha pulled back and gave him a hard look. "Never let them see you sweat," she told him. Flo quickly gathered himself. Sasha then made eye contact with her sister Veronica. She gave her a long look.

"Hi, Sasha," Veronica spoke braking the ice.

"Hello, to you too sister," Sasha stated with a look that Veronica couldn't detect. Everyone began to greet Sasha. Omar was amongst one of the happiest people to actually see Sasha again.

"Man, the streets miss you!" he stated hugging her. The Marshall cleared his throat breaking their moment up.

Someone tweeted that Sasha was at the funeral and the internet started going into a frenzy.

"A real Queen bitch back," someone tweeted.

"Uh oh, the streets in trouble," someone else tweeted.

"I'm on my way, pull up game strong," another person tweeted and the tweets went on and on.

She was the people's champ, they literary worship the ground she walked on. She fed a lot of families. People started pulling up to the funeral just to get a glimpse of her. Sasha proceeded toward the casket, she inspected the picture that was beside it.

'My babies have grown so much while I was away,' she thought. She bowed her head and began to say a prayer. In mid prayer she heard the double doors opened and looked back with an interesting look on her face. In walked Stevo, Kiesha, and Rick Rick. The air was thick with tension, everyone knew about the war that was going on so seeing the DIME-BOYZ all in one room together only amounted to one thing, trouble.

Shootsum and Dee Dee stood up, Kill was using the rest room. Flo began advancing toward Stevo.

*'This bitch ass nigga got the nerves,'* Flo thought temper flaring. Seeing the look on his face made Sasha frown, and she put a hand on his chest stopping him in his tracks.

"I come in peace," Stevo spoke.

"You have five seconds to get the fuck outta here," Flo spoke forgetting he was in a church.

"That's our brother laying in that casket and we just came to show our respect," Stevo stated.

"Nigga, get yo soft ass out before I beat yo ass bitch nigga," Flo stated.

"That's enough Flo," Sasha Stated. "We not having none of this shit here today, this here is about Valo, if you niggas don't dead that shit imma slap the shit out of both of y'all," she stated with authority. Even tho she was in hand cuffs they still didn't take the threat lightly.

"They are not welcomed here Sasha," Dee Dee spoke.

"Bitch nobody asked you," Kiesha jumped in defending her gang.

"You see a bitch smack a bitch," Dee Dee stated.

Sasha looked at the women, *'what the fuck is going on,'* she thought unaware of the ongoing beef. Pastor Jenkins sensed what was going on and walked over to intervene. Everyone there was watching the exchange, some was even grabbing their purse thinking about heading out before shit got outta control. Kill walked out of the rest room and saw the DIME-BOYZ.

*'What the fuck, how these niggas get in?'* he thought seeing Rick Rick, Keisha, and Stevo. He didn't recognized Sasha. They were all standing next to the casket.

"This nigga shot me and have the nerves to show up at bruh funeral like shit sweet, fuck niggas think this is I'm from Milwaukee." Kill snuck up behind Rick Rick and caught him with a hard-right hook almost knocking him to the ground. All hell broke loose.

Seeing this, Stevo caught Kill with a three-punch combination knocking him to the ground. Flo tried to rush Stevo but Kiesha tripped him causing Dee Dee to catch her with a two-piece spicy. Kiesha recovered quickly and counter with a two piece of her on knocking Dee Dee into Veronica. Queena pushed Dee Dee off of her mom. Dee Dee licked her lips and tasted blood.

*'I'm about to kill this bitch,'* DeeDee thought. Flo got up and him and Stevo began going blow for blow just like they did when they were kids. Stevo began to get the best of him until Shootsum grabbed him in the choke hold. Rick Rick tackled him causing him to stumble. It was like slow motion as he stumbled into Valo's casket causing it to slowly tip over. Everybody stopped fighting and looked. The casket fell on its side causing the door to opened on impact, everybody gasped.

They couldn't believe their eyes, Sasha grabbed her chest, Veronica and Queena covered their mouth. Stevo and Flo both frowned while the pastor dropped the microphone, he couldn't believe it. Valo, where was he because the casket… the casket… it was empty….

# To Be continued
# On Foe' Nem Grave: Part II

# Acknowledgements

First things first, I want to thank God for giving me the gift and the ability to write. Anything's possible if you put God first. Secondly, I want to thank my Baby Cakes. If amazing was a person! You literary came into my life and showed me how a woman could bring the best out of a man. I love and appreciate you for everything you do for me, you make me a better person. To my daughters Kiah and Beauty, I love you both. You two inspire and motivate me like only you two could. Shout out to my sisters and brothers, and my Pops Devail. My Granny, love you Granny and my whole support system... love you all. My TT Betty, love you... you know you're the best TT in the world. Special shout out to Kendrick Watkins and the whole So You Can Write Publications staffing crew. I love their system and how much they care about their work. They're so hands on and available which makes me so comfortable. Thanks. They made this process so easy for me. To everyone I missed, you know it's all love, and I hope you enjoy the book.... Oh, yeah, part two coming soon.

*Best Kept Secret*

"Where the writers go…"
www.sycwp.com